MENTAL TOUGHNESS FOR YOUNG ATHLETES UNLEASHED

PRACTICAL YOUTH SPORTS PSYCHOLOGY STRATEGIES FOR MINDSET TRAINING TO INSTANTLY BOOST FOCUS, RESILIENCE, AND CONFIDENCE IN JUST MINUTES A DAY

RUSH HEMPHILL PT, DPT, CSCS

SPEAR PUBLISHING LLC

© COPYRIGHT [SPEAR PUBLISHING LLC] [2024] - ALL RIGHTS RESERVED.

The content within this book may not be reproduced, duplicated or transmitted without direct written permission from the author or the publisher.

Under no circumstances will any blame or legal responsibility be held against the publisher, or author, for any damages, reparation, or monetary loss due to the information contained within this book. Either directly or indirectly. You are responsible for your own choices, actions, and results.

LEGAL NOTICE:

This book is copyright protected. This book is only for personal use. You cannot amend, distribute, sell, use, quote or paraphrase any part, of the content within this book, without the consent of the author or publisher.

DISCLAIMER NOTICE:

Please note the information contained within this document is for educational and entertainment purposes only. All effort has been expended to present accurate, up-to-date, and reliable, complete information. No warranties of any kind are declared or implied. Readers acknowledge that the author is not engaging in the rendering of legal, financial, medical or professional advice. The content within this book has been derived from various sources. Please consult a licensed professional before attempting any techniques outlined in this book.

By reading this document, the reader agrees that under no circumstances is the author responsible for any losses, direct or indirect, which are incurred as a result of the use of the information contained within this document, including, but not limited to, — errors, omissions, or inaccuracies.

CONTENTS

Introduction — vii

1. Laying the Foundation of Mental Toughness — 1
2. Developing Focus and Concentration — 13
3. Managing Stress and Anxiety — 27
4. Building and Sustaining Confidence — 39
5. Cultivating Resilience and Grit — 51
6. Balancing Athletics with Life — 65
7. Advanced Mental Training Techniques — 79
8. Nutrition, Rest, and Mental Performance — 93
9. Parent and Coach Support Strategies — 107
10. Putting It All Together: Strategies for Continuous Improvement — 119

Conclusion — 127

Bibliography — 129
About the Author — 133
Also by Rush Hemphill — 135

UNLOCK YOUR ATHLETIC POTENTIAL

Discover How to Boost Your Focus, Confidence, and Resilience in Just 10 Minutes a Day!

Are you a young athlete striving to perform at your best, both on and off the field? Do you struggle with staying focused during games, bouncing back from setbacks, or managing stress under pressure?

Imagine if you had the tools to overcome those challenges with ease —to feel more confident, stay cool in high-stakes moments, and unlock the resilience needed to push through the toughest days.

INTRODUCING THE MENTAL TOUGHNESS WORKSHEET FOR YOUNG ATHLETES

This FREE worksheet is packed with step-by-step actions designed to help you:

- **Strengthen Your Focus** so distractions no longer hold you back
- **Build Resilience** to bounce back from setbacks stronger than ever
- **Master Positive Self-Talk** to turn your doubts into motivation
- **Develop a Pre-Game Routine** that sets you up for success
- **Manage Stress and Anxiety** with powerful breathing techniques

What You'll Get:

- **Easy-to-Follow Steps**: No complicated jargon. Just clear, easy actionable steps to help you stay on top of your mental game.
- **Proven Techniques**: These methods are used by elite athletes to enhance their focus, confidence, and performance.
- **10-Minute Daily Routine**: You don't need hours of training—just a few minutes a day to start seeing results.

WHY MENTAL TOUGHNESS IS THE KEY TO SUCCESS

Physical strength is only part of the game. **Mental toughness** is the edge that separates good athletes from great ones. Whether you're battling the nerves before a big competition or trying to shake off a bad game, the right mindset can make all the difference.

Don't let stress, self-doubt, or distractions hold you back. With this worksheet, you'll develop the skills you need to stay calm, focused, and confident when it matters most.

Ready to Take Your Game to the Next Level?

This worksheet is designed to complement the strategies laid out in this book, *Mental Toughness for Young Athletes Unleashed*. It's **your FREE guide** to starting the journey toward mastering your mind and maximizing your potential.

Get Instant Access to the FREE Mental Toughness Worksheet Now! Scan the QR code to get your FREE Worksheet!

Download Your Free Worksheet Now!

Don't wait—your competition isn't. **Start developing the mental toughness that champions are made of.**

INTRODUCTION

Did you know that over 70% of young athletes report feeling significant stress and anxiety due to performance pressures? How do you currently manage the mental demands of your sport?

My name is Rush Hemphill, and through my career as a physical therapist, personal trainer, and former athlete, I have witnessed firsthand the critical role mental toughness plays in athletic performance. It is not only important for athletes to work on strength and conditioning and rehab, but also build the mental resilience needed to excel in sports and life.

This book is crafted with the intention to arm you—a young athlete, coach, or parent—with a straightforward process designed to fortify mental toughness. The aim is clear: enhance your performance in sports and every facet of your life by cultivating a resilient, focused, and adaptable mindset.

Mental toughness is not just about pushing through hard times; it's about thriving in the face of challenges. Athletes who develop mental resilience perform better, enjoy their sport more and have higher levels of overall well-being. This will give you the extra edge over your competition that neglects this area.

Throughout this book, we will explore the nature of mental toughness. We will start by understanding its foundations and then explore practical strategies for its development and ways to sustain it. Each section is structured to build on the previous one, creating a comprehensive journey from theory to practice.

This book speaks directly to you—the driven high school athlete, the collegiate competitor aiming for the top, the dedicated coach, and the supportive parent. It is designed to address the unique pressures you face and provide you with tools that are not only applicable on the field but also beneficial in academics, work, and personal relationships.

Let me share a quick personal story. Early in my career, I worked with a young baseball athletes who often struggled with game day nerves or self-confidence. Through tailored mental and physical conditioning, not only did physical capabilities improve, but newfound confidence also propelled these athletes to new heights in all areas of life. This journey inspired me to write this book and help others in similar situations.

What sets this guide apart is its holistic approach and real world examples. We won't just talk about improving your game-time performance; we'll also discuss how these strategies can help you succeed in the classroom, grow in your faith, and strengthen family bonds.

I invite you to join me on this transformative journey. Let's take the first step together towards unlocking your true potential by building a robust mental game.

Remember, developing mental toughness is a skill, and like any skill, it can be learned and mastered. With the right guidance and a commitment to practice, you are already on your path to greatness. Let's get started.

CHAPTER 1
LAYING THE FOUNDATION OF MENTAL TOUGHNESS

"Champions aren't made in gyms. Champions are made from something they have deep inside them—a desire, a dream, a vision."
– Muhammad Ali

AS A YOUNG ATHLETE, you know the thrill of pushing your limits and the satisfaction of achieving a personal best. Yet, behind every physical display of strength and endurance lies an equally critical, though less visible, force: mental toughness. Whether it's the final minutes of a tightly contested game or balancing the demands of school and training, mental toughness is your secret weapon. But what exactly does it mean to be mentally tough, especially for an athlete like you?

In sports, we often celebrate physical prowess, but the mental aspect often determines who truly excels and who folds under pressure. By understanding and developing your mental toughness, you will be better equipped to handle the inevitable challenges that come both on and off the field. This chapter will guide you through the foundational aspects of mental toughness, setting the stage for deeper exploration and practical application in subsequent chapters.

DEFINING MENTAL TOUGHNESS IN THE CONTEXT OF YOUTH SPORTS

Mental toughness is often hailed as a critical determinant of success in youth sports, but its definition can be elusive. For young athletes like you, mental toughness isn't just about enduring a tough training session or persisting through a game; it's about consistently managing and excelling under the pressures of competition, training, and life balance.

Unlike physical toughness, which is often visible and quantifiable, mental toughness involves a more subtle set of skills. It encompasses psychological resilience—the ability to bounce back from setbacks and failures with even greater strength and wisdom. It's about emotional control, maintaining composure in the face of frustration or excitement, which keeps you performing at your best.

Consider the example of a high school basketball player who missed a crucial shot during a major game, leading to his team's defeat. Instead of spiraling into self-doubt, he used the experience to fuel his practice sessions, focusing on his shooting skills and mental preparation for handling high-pressure moments. His determination not to be defined by a single failure is a prime example of mental toughness. The following season, he was not only the team's top scorer but also the most reliable player in clutch situations.

The key attributes of mental toughness include:

- Focus: allows you to concentrate on the task at hand while blocking out distractions.
- Determination: drives you to persevere despite difficulties.
- The ability to rebound from setbacks: viewing them as temporary and learning from each experience.

These qualities ensure that you are not merely enduring your challenges but are actively learning from them and using them to propel yourself forward.

Understanding and cultivating these attributes will not only enhance your performance in sports but will also empower you to navigate the complexities of daily life with confidence and poise. As we continue, remember that mental toughness is not an innate trait but a skill that can be developed and refined over time with practice and commitment.

THE ROLE OF SELF-ASSESSMENT IN IDENTIFYING MENTAL STRENGTHS AND WEAKNESSES

In the realm of sports, where physical abilities often steal the spotlight, understanding and honing your mental game can significantly elevate your performance. This begins with self-assessment—a crucial yet often overlooked aspect of athletic development. Self-assessment allows you, the athlete, to gain insights into your mental strengths and weaknesses, crafting a clearer path toward personal excellence. Let's explore how various tools and methods can aid in this essential practice.

Self-assessment in sports isn't just about reflecting on your physical performance; it extends deeply into evaluating your psychological state and responses to various situations. One effective tool is maintaining a performance journal. Here, you document not only the outcomes and statistics of your performances but also your emotional responses and the mental strategies you employed during those performances. For instance, noting how you felt during a pivotal moment in a game and what your thought process was can help you understand whether it was your mental state that influenced the outcome. This practice encourages a routine of mindfulness and self-awareness that is crucial for mental growth.

Feedback from coaches and teammates also plays a pivotal role in self-assessment. While self-reflection provides you with internal insights, external feedback offers an outsider's perspective on your mental toughness. For example, a coach might notice that your performance dips under certain pressures that you might not recognize yourself. Combining these insights with your personal reflections offers a more rounded view of where your mental toughness stands and what needs to be worked on.

Moreover, psychological tests designed specifically for athletes can unveil deeper layers of your psyche, revealing traits such as your response to competition, resilience, and ability to focus. These tests, often administered by sports psychologists, can provide a baseline of your mental attributes, which is invaluable in tracking your progress over time.

The importance of honest evaluation in this process cannot be overstated. It's easy to shy away from acknowledging our weaknesses, but true growth comes from facing them head-on. Honesty in your self-assessments allows you to make precise adjustments to your training, strategies, and mental approach. It's not just about working harder but about working smarter, using your self-knowledge to fine-tune your approach in both practice and competition.

From these assessments, you can develop a personal development plan that is uniquely tailored to your needs. This plan isn't just a schedule of physical training but includes mental skills training, psychological exercises, and regular reassessment points. For instance, if your self-assessment reveals a tendency to lose focus under pressure, your development plan might include specific exercises to enhance concentration, such as meditation or cognitive drills, and set checkpoints to evaluate improvement. Similarly, if resilience is identified as a weakness, your plan might incorporate scenarios and simulations that gradually expose you to stress, helping you build a tougher mental stance over time.

The continuous loop of assessment, feedback, and adjustment is what ultimately cultivates a stronger, more resilient athlete. By regularly engaging in these practices, you become more attuned to your mental needs and more adept at navigating the mental challenges of competitive sports. This proactive approach to mental training ensures that your development is constant, keeping you competitive and mentally sharp.

In integrating these self-assessment tools into your routine, remember the objective is not to criticize or undervalue your abilities but to illuminate the path towards greater mental toughness and, consequently, superior athletic performance. By embracing this reflective practice, you set the stage for not just incremental improvements but transformative growth in your sports career and beyond.

SETTING REALISTIC GOALS: THE FIRST STEP TO BUILDING CONFIDENCE

In the arena of competitive sports, the ability to set and achieve goals is not just a tool—it's a fundamental skill that every young athlete must cultivate to excel. Establishing realistic, well-defined goals is like drawing a map for your athletic journey; it gives you direction, keeps you motivated, and boosts your confidence as you chart your progress. Let's delve into how you can harness the power of goal setting to elevate your sports performance and personal growth.

The SMART criteria offers a robust framework for setting effective goals. SMART stands for Specific, Measurable, Achievable, Relevant, and Time-bound. Each element plays a crucial role in ensuring the goals you set are not only clear but also attainable and aligned with your long-term aspirations. For young athletes, making your goals Specific means clearly defining what you want to achieve, such as improving your sprint speed, RBI, or increasing your free-throw accuracy. Measurable goals have quantifiable indicators, allowing you to track your progress. For instance, rather than merely aiming to 'improve your sprint speed,' a measurable goal would be 'to reduce your 100-meter dash time by 0.5 seconds within three months.'

Achievability is about ensuring that the goal is within your reach, considering your current abilities and constraints. This doesn't mean you shouldn't aim high, but your goals should challenge you realistically based on your current skill level and resources. Relevance ensures that the goals are meaningful to you and directly impact your sports performance or personal development. Finally, Time-bound goals have a deadline, which creates a sense of urgency and helps you organize your efforts more effectively.

Setting incremental goals is equally important. These are smaller, short-term objectives that lead you step-by-step towards your larger, long-term ambitions. For example, if a collegiate basketball player aims to improve their shooting accuracy, an incremental goal could be to increase their shooting practice to an additional hour per week, focusing specifically on free throws. Another short-term goal might be to seek feedback from a coach or watch tutorial videos to understand shooting mechanics better. These smaller steps are manageable and less daunting than the overarching goal, maintaining focus and motivation as you gradually see tangible improvements.

To illustrate, consider a high school swimmer aiming to qualify for a national competition. The swimmer's long-term goal is to cut their 200-meter freestyle time by four seconds by the end of the season. Incremental goals might include improving flip turn techniques, enhancing stamina through targeted workouts, and participating in monthly regional competitions to gain experience. Each of these smaller goals contributes to the larger objective, and achieving them provides frequent boosts of confidence and a sense of accomplishment.

Achieving these smaller, incremental goals plays a critical role in building an athlete's confidence. Confidence in sports, as in life, stems from demonstrated ability and success. Each time you reach a goal, no matter how small, it serves as proof of your capabilities, reinforcing your self-belief. This confidence then fuels further efforts, creating a positive cycle of growth and achievement. For instance, a young tennis player who sets the goal to master a new serving technique and achieves it within the desired timeframe is likely to feel more confident not only in their serve but in their ability to master other techniques as well.

In practice, the process of setting and achieving goals should be dynamic. As you grow and your circumstances change, so too should your goals. Regularly revisiting and revising your goals ensures they remain challenging yet achievable, keeping you aligned with your evolving aspirations and capabilities. This dynamic approach to goal setting not only maximizes your development as an athlete but also instills a lifelong skill that transcends sports, equipping you to tackle the broader goals of your academic, personal, and professional life.

UNDERSTANDING THE MIND-BODY CONNECTION IN YOUNG ATHLETES

The interplay between the mind and body is a crucial yet often overlooked aspect of athletic performance. As young athletes, recognizing how your mental states can influence your physical capabilities—and vice versa—provides a significant advantage. It's well-understood that psychological factors such as stress, anxiety, and focus can directly impact physical performance. Conversely, physical states can affect mental well-being. For instance, regular physical activity is known to reduce symptoms of depression and anxiety, enhancing overall mental health. This reciprocal relationship forms the core of the mind-body connection in sports.

Let's delve deeper into how this connection plays out on the field or court. Imagine a scenario where you're about to take a crucial penalty shot. Your heart races, your palms sweat, and a barrage of thoughts cloud your mind—both positive and negative. Here, your mental state directly influences your physical reaction: muscle tension, breathing rate, and coordination. Successful athletes learn to manage these mental reactions to maintain optimal physical performance during critical moments. Conversely, being in peak physical condition can boost your mental clarity and confidence, further illustrating the symbiotic relationship between mind and body.

To enhance this connection, several techniques can be employed, with Yoga, meditation, and breathing exercises being among the most effective. Yoga, for instance, is not just about physical flexibility and strength; its practices are deeply rooted in integrating mental focus with physical movements, enhancing overall mindfulness and body awareness. Regular yoga practice helps athletes gain better control over their breathing and body alignment, which can translate into improved performance and reduced injury risk.

Mipan, a well-known yoga instructor and former athlete, underscores the value of Yoga in sports: "Yoga teaches you how to listen to your body, to understand its signals, and to respond appropriately. This awareness is crucial not just in performing better but also in preventing injuries." This perspective is supported by numerous studies, one of which demonstrated that athletes who incorporated Yoga into their training regimen experienced improved balance, enhanced concentration, and a significant reduction in sports-related injuries.

Meditation, particularly mindfulness meditation, is another powerful tool for strengthening the mind-body connection. It involves sitting quietly and paying attention to thoughts, sounds, the sensations of breathing, or parts of the body, bringing your mind's attention to the present without drifting into concerns about the past or future. This practice enhances your ability to concentrate under pressure, a vital skill during competitions. For example, a study published in the 'Journal of Cognitive Enhancement' found that athletes who practiced mindfulness meditation showed significant improvements in their ability to focus, remain calm, and recover from performance errors more quickly.

Breathing exercises also play a pivotal role in fortifying the mind-body nexus. Techniques such as diaphragmatic breathing not only help in regulating your breath during intense physical exertion but also calm the mind, reducing performance anxiety. These exercises can be particularly beneficial before a competition, helping you center your focus and manage adrenaline. Practical exercises include the '4-7-8 technique', where you breathe in for four seconds, hold the breath for seven seconds, and exhale for eight seconds. This method not only improves lung function but also triggers an automatic nervous system response that relaxes the body, ideal for high-stress sports scenarios.

Incorporating these techniques into your training regimen doesn't require extensive alterations to your existing schedule. Starting with as little as five minutes of meditation or Yoga at the beginning or end of your daily training can yield significant benefits. Over time, these practices enhance your mental resilience and physical performance, creating a robust athlete who excels under pressure. As you continue to train and compete, keep in mind that the strength of your mind-body connection can be the key differentiator between good and great athletes.

THE IMPORTANCE OF RESILIENCE: LESSONS FROM YOUNG CHAMPIONS

Resilience in youth sports is the ability to bounce back from setbacks, adapt to challenges, and keep moving forward in the face of adversity. For young athletes, this isn't just about recovering from a loss or a bad play; it's about handling the highs and lows of sports with grace, maintaining a steadfast dedication regardless of the situation, and continually striving to improve. Resilience is critical because sports, by nature, are filled with challenges that can either serve as stepping stones or stumbling blocks. The difference lies in how an athlete confronts these obstacles.

Let's consider the stories of young athletes who have faced significant challenges yet emerged stronger. Take the case of a high school soccer player who tore her ACL during a pivotal match. Despite this severe injury, her spirit remained unbroken. Post-surgery, her journey back to the field was grueling, filled with strenuous rehab and slow progress. However, her resolve didn't waver. She attended every team practice, albeit as a spectator initially, and used visualization techniques to keep her mind sharp and engaged. She imagined herself executing perfect passes and scoring goals. Over time, her physical capabilities began to align with her mental rehearsals. By the next season, not only was she back as her team's starting forward, but she also led them to a regional championship. Her ability to mentally engage with her sport, even when physically sidelined, showcases the power of resilience.

Another example is a young swimmer who consistently finished behind his peers, struggling to make a mark in competitions. Instead of succumbing to frustration, he used positive self-talk to bolster his spirits. He would remind himself of his love for swimming and his improving techniques rather than focusing solely on the outcome of races. This shift in perspective from outcome to growth and enjoyment fueled his persistence. Over time, his performance improved, and eventually, he qualified for state-level championships. His story underscores that resilience is often built in small increments, fostered by a positive mindset and an unwavering focus on personal progress.

Young athletes can employ several effective strategies to build resilience. Visualization, as seen in the soccer player's story, involves picturing oneself succeeding in various scenarios and can enhance both physical and mental readiness. Positive self-talk, which helped the swimmer, involves replacing negative thoughts with encouraging and affirming statements. This practice not only boosts confidence but also redirects the athlete's focus from fear of failure to a mindset of growth and possibility.

Stress management also plays a key role in developing resilience. Techniques such as deep breathing exercises, progressive muscle relaxation, and mindfulness can help athletes manage their stress levels effectively. These practices not only improve focus and performance under pressure but also enhance overall well-being, making athletes more resilient in facing both the physical and mental demands of their sports.

The link between resilience and long-term success in sports—and life—is undeniable. Resilient athletes are more likely to view challenges as opportunities for growth, pushing them to strive higher and dig deeper. Their ability to recover from setbacks also prepares them for the unpredictability of competitions and the rigors of training. In addition, the skills learned through developing resilience, such as emotional regulation, stress management, and optimistic thinking, are invaluable life skills. These skills equip young athletes to handle academic pressures, personal relationships, and future career challenges with a balanced and proactive approach.

In essence, resilience in sports transcends the immediate recovery from a physical setback or a poor performance. It involves a holistic strengthening of the mind and character, enabling young athletes to navigate the ups and downs of their sporting careers with determination and grace. As we continue to explore the components of mental toughness, remember that resilience is not just about bouncing back; it's also about moving forward with a clearer vision and a stronger heart.

CHAPTER 2
DEVELOPING FOCUS AND CONCENTRATION

"The successful warrior is the average man, with laser-like focus."
– Bruce Lee

IMAGINE STANDING at the free-throw line, the buzz of the crowd a mere murmur in the back of your mind. You have just seconds to make the shot that could win the game. At this moment, the ability to zero in on your task with laser-like focus is what separates good athletes from great ones. Focus and concentration in sports are not just about blocking out noise; they are about honing your mental acuity to enhance performance under pressure and training conditions. This chapter is designed to equip you with practical techniques and exercises to sharpen your mental focus, helping you perform at your best when it counts the most.

TECHNIQUES FOR IMPROVING CONCENTRATION DURING TRAINING AND COMPETITIONS

CONCENTRATION EXERCISES

One effective method to enhance your concentration is through specific exercises that train your mind to focus intensely. Consider the 'focus grid' exercise, a tool used by many coaches to improve athletes' visual concentration and attention to detail. A focus grid involves a large grid of numbers or letters, and the challenge is to find sequences or patterns as quickly as possible under time pressure. This exercise not only sharpens your visual focus but also enhances your ability to stay concentrated under stress, mimicking the quick decision-making required in sports.

Another valuable exercise is the 'concentration countdown.' This involves choosing a complex object and focusing all your attention on it for a prolonged period, typically several minutes. The goal is to notice as many details as possible without allowing your mind to wander. If distractions intrude, you start the countdown again. Regular practice of this exercise can significantly enhance your ability to maintain deep focus, which is essential during both training and competitive events.

USE OF CUE WORDS

Cue words are short, powerful reminders that bring your focus back to the present moment during both training and competitions. These words or brief phrases should be motivational and connected to your performance goals. For instance, a runner might use the cue word "smooth" to remind themselves to keep their stride relaxed and efficient. During moments of high pressure or distraction, mentally repeating this cue word can refocus your mind on your running technique rather than on the stress of the race.

The effectiveness of cue words lies in their ability to act as anchors, keeping you grounded in the present and focused on what you can control. They should be practiced during training so that during competitions, these words automatically bring your focus back without conscious effort.

SIMULATE HIGH-PRESSURE SCENARIOS

To excel in sports, you must be able to maintain concentration under the intense pressure of competition. One way to develop this skill is to simulate high-pressure scenarios during your training sessions. For example, if you are a basketball player, your coach might set up a situation where you need to make several free throws in a row while your teammates create distractions. These simulations should mimic the actual challenges you face during competitions, allowing you to practice maintaining focus in disruptive environments.

Regular exposure to these controlled high-pressure situations will make you more comfortable when you inevitably face them in real competitions. The more you practice, the better your concentration will be when it really counts.

REGULAR ASSESSMENT AND FEEDBACK

Improving concentration is an ongoing process that requires regular assessment and feedback. It's important to continuously evaluate how well you are maintaining focus during both practices and competitions. Feedback from coaches can be invaluable in identifying when your concentration wavers and understanding what may be causing these lapses.

Coaches can use video recordings of games and training sessions to review and point out moments where your attention might have slipped, providing concrete examples to learn from. These sessions can also help identify patterns or specific conditions under which your concentration needs improvement.

You can make targeted improvements by continually assessing your ability to concentrate and integrating feedback into your training.

This proactive approach ensures that your training is always aligned with your evolving needs as an athlete, helping you refine your focus and concentration to the point where they become second nature during your performances.

As we move forward, remember that the ability to concentrate and maintain focus under pressure is not just a skill but a competitive advantage that can set you apart from your peers. The techniques outlined here are just the beginning. With dedication and regular practice, you can see significant improvements in your ability to focus, which will translate into better performance in your sport and beyond.

THE ART OF MAINTAINING FOCUS AMIDST DISTRACTIONS

Distractions, whether internal, like a flurry of anxiety, or external, such as the roar of a crowd, pose significant challenges to maintaining focus during athletic performances. As an athlete, understanding these distractions and developing strategies to manage them is crucial for maintaining optimal performance. Internal distractions often stem from nerves, negative thoughts, or performance pressure. External distractions can include audience noise, weather conditions, or even unexpected changes in the game schedule. To handle these effectively, you must first identify and then develop tailored strategies to keep your focus sharp.

For internal distractions like anxiety, a practical approach is to implement relaxation techniques right before and during competitions. Techniques such as deep breathing or progressive muscle relaxation can help calm your mind and reduce the physical symptoms of anxiety, such as elevated heartbeat and tension. Establishing a pre-performance routine that includes these techniques can make them more effective. One effective strategy for external distractions is using controlled exposure during training. For instance, practicing in noisy environments or varying practice times can help you acclimate to different conditions you might face during actual competitions, making you less susceptible to being thrown off by them during crucial moments.

Moreover, integrating mental rehearsals into your training can prepare you for dealing with distractions. By visualizing yourself succeeding in spite of distractions, you reinforce your ability to remain focused no matter the external conditions. This mental practice not only boosts confidence but also enhances your ability to concentrate when it counts.

TRAINING IN DIVERSE ENVIRONMENTS

To further hone your ability to maintain focus amidst distractions, it's beneficial to train in a variety of environments. This strategy prepares you for the unpredictable nature of sports settings and enhances your adaptability and mental toughness. For example, suppose you're used to training in a quiet, controlled environment. In that case, occasional sessions in a more chaotic, noisy setting can be very beneficial. This could mean practicing your drills on a busy field or participating in practice matches with crowd noise played over speakers.

Such diverse training environments challenge you to maintain focus despite the chaos, mirroring competition conditions where distractions are inevitable. Over time, training in these varied environments will help you develop a robust ability to concentrate, making you less likely to be disrupted by unexpected conditions during key events. This approach encourages a mindset that views distractions as part of the game rather than obstacles, which is crucial for mental resilience in sports.

FOCUS DRILLS

Specific focus drills can also greatly enhance your ability to maintain concentration. One effective drill is the 'single-task focus' practice, where you concentrate solely on one aspect of your performance at a time. For instance, a tennis player might focus exclusively on their serve during a practice session, ignoring all other elements of their game momentarily. This drill trains the brain to channel all energy and attention into one task, fostering a high level of concentration that can be critical during competitive play.

By regularly integrating these single-task focus drills into your training routine, you develop the skill to switch your focus on demand, which is invaluable during competitions where you might need to rapidly shift your attention between different tasks, such as adjusting from defense to attack in team sports.

MENTAL CONDITIONING GAMES

Incorporating mental conditioning games and apps designed to enhance focus can also be a fun and effective way to reduce susceptibility to distractions. These tools are designed to train your brain in much the same way you train your body, strengthening your mental faculties through regular practice. Games that require quick responses or involve complex problem-solving under time pressure can be particularly effective. These activities sharpen your cognitive abilities, improving your reaction times and your ability to stay focused under stress.

Apps like Lumosity or Peak offer games specifically designed to improve attention and concentration, and they can be a great addition to your mental training arsenal. Regularly using these apps for short periods—perhaps as a warm-up before physical training sessions—can lead to significant improvements in your ability to focus during both training and competitions. By turning focus training into a challenging and enjoyable activity, you're more likely to commit to regular practice, leading to better concentration when you need it most.

Through understanding and practicing these strategies—recognizing distractions, training in diverse environments, employing focus drills, and engaging with mental conditioning games—you can significantly enhance your ability to maintain concentration, no matter the distractions you face. This skill is not just about improving sports performance; it's about cultivating a mental edge that will serve you well across all areas of life, from the playing field to the classroom and beyond.

MINDFULNESS PRACTICES TAILORED FOR YOUNG ATHLETES

In the fast-paced world of sports, where every second counts, the ability to stay present and fully engaged during both training and competition can significantly enhance an athlete's performance. Mindfulness, a practice rooted in being intensely aware of what you're sensing and feeling at every moment without interpretation or judgment, can be a game-changer for young athletes like you. By incorporating basic mindfulness exercises into your routine, you can develop a sharper focus, control stress, and improve your overall athletic performance.

BASIC MINDFULNESS EXERCISES

Let's start with some simple yet effective mindfulness exercises designed specifically for athletes. Mindful breathing, for instance, is a foundational practice that involves focusing your attention on your breath, an action that you can control and monitor throughout your training or in a high-stress competition. Here's how you can practice it: Find a quiet spot and sit comfortably with your back straight. Close your eyes and take a few deep breaths to settle in. Then, slowly shift your focus to your natural breathing pattern. Notice the air entering through your nostrils, filling your lungs, and leaving your body. If your mind wanders, gently guide it back to your breath. This practice not only helps in reducing performance anxiety but also sharpens your focus, preparing you mentally before a game or helping you regain concentration during a tense moment.

Another beneficial mindfulness technique is the body scan. This involves mentally scanning your body from head to toe, observing sensations of pain, tension, warmth, or relaxation without trying to change them. Start by focusing on the sensations in your feet and slowly move your attention up to your head. If you find areas of tension, acknowledge them and imagine breathing into them to release the tightness. This exercise is particularly useful after training sessions as it increases your awareness of how different parts of your body are feeling, which can be crucial for injury prevention and recovery.

APPLICATION IN DAILY TRAINING

Integrating mindfulness into your daily training might seem challenging at first, but with consistency, it becomes a natural part of your routine. Start by dedicating a few minutes at the beginning or end of your training sessions to practice mindful breathing or a body scan. This not only sets a calm, focused tone for the training session but also helps mentally condition you to stay present and engaged. Gradually, you can start incorporating mindfulness into the actual training exercises. For instance, when running drills, focus fully on each step, each breath, and each movement, observing how your body feels and how it responds to different actions. This heightened awareness can lead to improvements in technique and performance as you become more attuned to the nuances of your body's responses.

BENEFITS OF REGULAR PRACTICE

The benefits of incorporating regular mindfulness practice into your training regimen are extensive. One of the most immediate effects is stress reduction. Mindfulness helps in lowering stress levels by enhancing your ability to manage and dissipate anxiety, which is especially beneficial before competitions. It can also lead to increased performance consistency. By training your mind to be present and focused, you reduce the likelihood of performance fluctuations, which are often caused by mental distractions or nerves. Over time, athletes who practice mindfulness report feeling more in control during competitions and more resilient in the face of adversity.

Regular mindfulness practice can enhance cognitive functions such as concentration, memory, and decision-making, all of which are crucial in sports. For example, a study published in the Journal of Clinical Sport Psychology found that athletes who engaged in consistent mindfulness training improved their attention and concentration levels significantly, leading to better performance outcomes in competitive sports.

MINDFUL RECOVERY

Mindfulness can play a crucial role in your recovery process. After intense training sessions or competitions, mindful recovery techniques can help you reset mentally and physically. Techniques like guided imagery, where you visualize a peaceful scene or a successful performance, can help shift your body into a rest-and-recover mode. This not only aids in physical recovery by reducing heart rate and muscle tension but also clears your mind of any residual stress or excitement from the performance.

Implementing these mindfulness practices regularly not only enhances your athletic performance but also contributes to a more balanced and fulfilling sporting experience. As you continue to train and compete, these techniques can become vital tools in your arsenal, helping you to manage the mental demands of sports with greater ease and effectiveness.

USING VISUALIZATION TO ENHANCE PERFORMANCE

Visualization, or mental imagery, is a powerful psychological tool that involves creating or recreating experiences in your mind. As a young athlete, learning to harness this technique can significantly amplify your performance by preparing you mentally for competition, enhancing your motivation, and even speeding up your recovery from injuries. Through visualization, you can mentally simulate specific aspects of your sport, from perfecting your technique to handling high-pressure situations effectively.

VISUALIZATION TECHNIQUES

There are several visualization techniques that can benefit you depending on your individual needs and the demands of your sport. One basic method is to visualize the perfect performance. Before a game or competition, close your eyes and imagine yourself executing every move flawlessly, from the start to the finish. Engage all your senses in this process—see the environment, hear the sounds, feel your movements, and experience the emotions of performing at your best. This technique can boost your confidence and mentally primes you to perform as visualized.

Another effective visualization technique focuses on overcoming obstacles during an event. Imagine different scenarios that could pose challenges during a performance, such as adverse weather conditions, a formidable opponent, or even making a mistake. Then, visualize yourself handling these challenges with composure and skill, adjusting your strategies, and maintaining your focus. This prepares you to remain calm and resourceful, turning potential disruptions into opportunities for demonstrating resilience and adaptability.

CREATING A VISUALIZATION ROUTINE

To get the most out of visualization:

1. Integrate it into your regular training routine.
2. Establish a consistent schedule for practicing visualization, ideally daily or several times a week.
3. Find a quiet place where you can relax without interruptions.
4. Start with just a few minutes per session, gradually increasing the duration as you become more comfortable with the process.

Your visualization routine should be tailored to your specific sporting events. For instance, if you are a swimmer, include images of diving off the blocks, the feeling of water against your skin, the sights and sounds of the pool, and the rhythm of your strokes. Be as detailed as possible to make the mental rehearsal as realistic as you can. Over time, this practice will enhance your mental clarity and focus during actual competitions, making the envisioned scenarios feel familiar and manageable.

EVIDENCE OF EFFECTIVENESS

Research supports the effectiveness of visualization in sports. Numerous studies have shown that mental practices can enhance muscle memory, improve confidence, and reduce anxiety levels in athletes. For example, a study published in the *Journal of Sport & Exercise Psychology* found that basketball players who used visualization techniques showed significant improvements in free-throw shooting performance.

These benefits are attributed to the way visualization activates the neural networks associated with actual physical performance. Mentally rehearsing your sport can stimulate the same neural pathways used during physical execution, enhancing your muscle memory and overall performance without additional physical strain.

SPORT-SPECIFIC SCENARIOS

To effectively apply visualization techniques, it's crucial to tailor your mental imagery to the specific demands of your sport. Here are some examples of visualization techniques for different sports:

- **Track and Field**: Visualize the entire sequence of a race—your start, the rhythm of your running, the feel of the track under your spikes, and the crowd cheering. Imagine executing perfect form and technique throughout the race and crossing the finish line ahead of others.
- **Soccer**: Imagine controlling the ball with precision, executing perfect passes, and scoring goals. Visualize different game scenarios, such as penalty kicks or defending against an aggressive opponent, seeing yourself succeed in each situation.

- **Gymnastics**: Picture yourself performing a routine flawlessly. Focus on each movement, the precision of your landings, and the strength of your executions. Feel the applause from the audience and the satisfaction of a well-executed performance.
- **Baseball**: Visualize yourself at bat, anticipating the pitch and making perfect contact with the ball. Imagine the crack of the bat, the trajectory of the ball soaring over the field, and rounding the bases with speed and precision. Picture yourself making pivotal plays in the field, such as catching a fly ball or throwing out a runner at home plate. Envision the crowd's roar and the feeling of accomplishment as you contribute to your team's victory.

By practicing sport-specific visualization, you create a mental blueprint that can guide your physical performance. The more vivid and accurate your visualizations are, the more effectively they can influence your actual performance, helping you to approach each competition with confidence and a clear mental image of success. This proactive mental preparation is a critical component of achieving excellence in sports. It can set you apart from your competitors, who may rely solely on physical training.

DEVELOPING A PRE-GAME ROUTINE THAT FOSTERS FOCUS

Creating an effective pre-game routine is crucial for any aspiring athlete. It serves as a mental and physical primer, setting the stage for optimal performance. By incorporating specific components such as warm-up exercises, mental rehearsal, and strategic planning into your routine, you can ensure that both your body and mind are finely tuned for the challenge ahead.

First, let's discuss the components that make up an effective pre-game routine. Warm-up exercises are essential not only to prepare your muscles but also to get your blood flowing, which enhances focus and sharpness. These should include a mix of dynamic stretches and sport-specific activities that activate the relevant muscle groups. For instance, a basketball player might include dribbling drills and free throws in their warm-up, while a swimmer might focus on dynamic stretches that mimic swimming strokes.

Mental rehearsal is another component that should not be overlooked. This involves visualizing your performance in the upcoming event, imagining yourself executing flawlessly, and responding adeptly to various scenarios. This practice not only boosts confidence but also prepares your mind for the task, making you mentally ready to engage with the competition. Strategic planning, on the other hand, involves going over your game plan and any specific strategies you intend to employ against your competitors. This might include reviewing tactical formations, set plays, or competitor analysis, ensuring that you step onto the field or court with a clear plan of action.

Personalizing your routine is key to making it effective. Each athlete is unique, with different needs and preferences that affect how they best prepare for a game. Therefore, it is important that you develop a routine that suits your specific requirements and complements your strengths. For example, suppose you are someone who gets particularly nervous before a competition. In that case, you might include more relaxation-focused exercises in your routine, such as deep breathing or listening to calming music. Conversely, if you tend to feel sluggish before a game, your routine might focus more on dynamic and energizing activities.

Coaches and mentors play a vital role in helping you develop and refine your pre-game routine. They can provide valuable feedback on what works and what doesn't, helping you to optimize each component of your routine. Coaches can also help you integrate mental and strategic elements into your routine, ensuring that you are physically and mentally prepared. Their experience and insight can be particularly useful in helping you adjust your routine based on different conditions and stages of your athletic development.

Following your pre-game routine consistently is crucial for its effectiveness. However, flexibility is also important. Being too rigid can make it difficult to adapt to unexpected situations, such as changes in scheduling or weather conditions. Therefore, while it is important to stick to your routine, you should also be prepared to modify it as needed. This balance between consistency and flexibility helps ensure that your routine always serves your best interests, allowing you to maintain focus and perform at your best no matter the circumstances.

A well-crafted pre-game routine is a fundamental tool that prepares you mentally and physically for competition. By understanding and implementing the key components of an effective routine, personalizing it to fit your specific needs, and working with coaches to refine it, you can enhance your focus and performance in any sporting event. Consistency in your routine builds familiarity and confidence, while flexibility allows you to adapt to any situation, ensuring that you are always prepared to give your best performance.

As we wrap up this chapter on developing focus and concentration, remember that the strategies discussed here are not just about immediate preparation but about cultivating habits that will enhance your mental toughness and focus in the long term. The next chapter will explore the crucial topic of managing stress and anxiety in sports, providing you with strategies to maintain your composure and perform under pressure. This is an essential aspect of mental toughness that complements the focus and concentration skills developed in this chapter, setting the stage for continued growth and excellence in your athletic endeavors.

CHAPTER 3
MANAGING STRESS AND ANXIETY

"Do not anticipate trouble or worry about what may never happen. Keep in the sunlight."
— Benjamin Franklin

IMAGINE you're seconds away from stepping onto the field or court. Your heart races, your palms sweat, and a whirlwind of thoughts cloud your mind. This moment is pivotal—not just in the game you're about to play but in your journey as an athlete. How you handle this surge of stress and anxiety can significantly influence your performance. Stress and anxiety in sports aren't just common; they are an integral part of the experience. However, managing them effectively can transform potential stumbling blocks into stepping stones towards success. This chapter delves into understanding and controlling the anxiety that accompanies athletic pursuits, ensuring you're equipped not just to cope but to thrive under pressure.

IDENTIFYING TRIGGERS OF ANXIETY IN SPORTS

Understand Personal Triggers

Every athlete is unique, with different aspects of competition and training that may trigger anxiety. For some, it might be the pressure of critical games; for others, high expectations from themselves or others, or perhaps memories of past failures loom large. The first step in managing your anxiety effectively is identifying these personal triggers. This understanding begins with keen observation and reflection on instances when you felt most anxious. Was it during a specific part of the game? Were there particular thoughts or situations that escalated your stress levels? Recognizing these triggers is crucial, as it allows you to address them directly through targeted strategies.

ROLE OF JOURNALING

Journaling is a powerful tool in the athlete's arsenal for managing stress and anxiety. By keeping a detailed journal of your training sessions, competitions, and how you felt before, during, and after, you can gain insights into the patterns and triggers of your anxiety. This record isn't just a log; it reflects your psychological state over time, providing clues on how different situations affect your mental health. When journaling, be as specific as possible—note what was going on, how you felt, what worked, and what didn't. Over time, this journal will become an invaluable resource for understanding and managing your sports-related anxiety.

EDUCATE ON COMMON TRIGGERS

While personal triggers vary, certain anxiety triggers are common among athletes. These include fear of injury, the pressure to perform, competition outcomes, and even interpersonal dynamics within a team. Understanding that these triggers are widespread can help you realize that you're not alone in your experience. Coaches and sports psychologists often work to make athletes aware of these common triggers, providing a framework within which they can understand their own experiences. Recognizing that others share similar challenges can also open up avenues for peer support, which is invaluable in managing stress and anxiety.

DEVELOP TRIGGER MANAGEMENT PLANS

Once you've identified your specific triggers, the next step is to develop management plans for each. This proactive approach involves creating strategies that you can employ before facing known stressors. For instance, if pre-game jitters are a major trigger, your plan might include a series of relaxation exercises and a pre-game routine that helps center your focus and calm your nerves. If the fear of failure triggers anxiety, setting realistic performance goals rather than outcome goals can help mitigate this. Your coach or a sports psychologist can assist in developing these plans, tailoring them to fit your individual needs and ensuring they are practical and effective.

Understanding and managing these triggers can significantly reduce the instances and intensity of anxiety, leading to improved performance and a more enjoyable athletic experience. Remember, the goal isn't to eliminate stress and anxiety completely—these emotions are natural and can even be motivating. Instead, the aim is to manage them effectively, ensuring they don't hinder your ability to perform your best.

Moving forward, we will explore specific techniques, such as breathing exercises and mental rehearsal strategies, that can further aid in managing stress and anxiety during competitions. These tools are not just about coping with negative emotions; they are about harnessing your inner strength to meet the challenges of sports with confidence and resilience.

BREATHING TECHNIQUES FOR IMMEDIATE STRESS RELIEF

In the heat of competition or even during intense training sessions, it's not uncommon to feel your heart racing and your breath quickening—physical manifestations of stress and anxiety that can impede your performance. This is where breathing techniques, specifically designed for quick stress relief and easy integration into your athletic routine, can be game-changers. By learning and applying methods such as diaphragmatic breathing, box breathing, and the 4-7-8 technique, you empower yourself with tools to regain control of your body's natural stress response, allowing you to maintain composure and focus when it counts most.

INTRODUCE BREATHING EXERCISES

Diaphragmatic breathing, often referred to as "deep breathing," involves full engagement of the diaphragm, a large muscle at the base of your lungs. Practicing this technique can help reduce the 'fight-or-flight' response, calming your nervous system and enhancing oxygen exchange—crucial during both physically and mentally demanding moments in sports. To practice, simply sit comfortably or lie flat, place one hand on your belly and the other on your chest, and inhale deeply through the nose so that your belly pushes against your hand while the chest remains relatively still. Exhale slowly through the mouth, engaging your abdominal muscles to complete the breath. This method not only helps in stress reduction but also improves lung capacity, which is beneficial for athletic endurance.

Box breathing, another effective technique, involves breathing in equal counts of four—inhale for four seconds, hold for four seconds, exhale for four seconds, and hold again for four seconds. This technique is particularly useful before or during a game or match as it helps maintain a rhythm that not only focuses the mind but also keeps the body in a state of calm readiness. The predictable pattern of box breathing can be a mental anchor during high-pressure moments, helping you stay centered and alert.

The 4-7-8 breathing technique, developed by Dr. Andrew Weil, is particularly effective in reducing anxiety quickly. To do this, you breathe in for four seconds, hold the breath for seven seconds, and exhale for eight seconds. This method helps to decrease anxiety, slow your heart rate, and regulate your body's stress response, which can be particularly useful during unexpected stressful situations in sports, such as a sudden point loss or a call against your team.

PRACTICAL APPLICATION DURING COMPETITION

Implementing these breathing techniques during competitions can be a subtle yet powerful way to manage stress. For instance, using diaphragmatic breathing during a timeout or a break can help lower your heart rate and clear your mind, preparing you for the next play. Similarly, if you find yourself overwhelmed by the crowd noise or the intensity of a close game, taking a moment for box breathing can provide an immediate calming effect, refocusing your mind and stabilizing your emotions.

Integrating these practices doesn't require special equipment or excessive time—it fits right into the brief pauses already built into most sports, such as the time between rounds, innings, or during halftime. The key is consistency and familiarity, which makes it easier to deploy these techniques effectively under pressure.

BENEFITS OF REGULAR PRACTICE

Incorporating these breathing exercises into your daily training regimen offers numerous benefits, extending beyond immediate stress relief. Regular practice can enhance your overall lung capacity and efficiency, which is vital for high-performance sports. It also trains your body to default to healthier breathing patterns under stress, improving your endurance and performance.

In addition, the calming effect of controlled breathing isn't just physical; it also contributes to mental clarity and emotional stability, which are crucial for making strategic decisions quickly and efficiently during games. Over time, these benefits contribute to a more focused, resilient athletic performance, giving you an edge over competitors who may not be as equipped to handle stress.

REAL-LIFE ATHLETE EXAMPLES

Consider the story of a collegiate sprinter who used breathing techniques to manage pre-race jitters. By practicing the 4-7-8 technique regularly, she was able to significantly reduce her anxiety, which had previously led to false starts and subpar performances. This simple change in her routine allowed her to start her races calm and focused, ultimately leading to her setting personal and school records.

Another example is a professional soccer player known for his penalty kick precision. He attributes his success to his pre-kick routine, which includes box breathing to center his focus and calm his nerves, allowing him to execute with precision even under immense pressure.

These athletes demonstrate that with the proper techniques and regular practice, managing stress through controlled breathing can become a vital part of an athlete's toolkit, enhancing performance and overall enjoyment of the sport.

PREPARING MENTALLY FOR HIGH-STAKES COMPETITIONS

When the stakes are high and the lights shine brightest, an athlete's mental preparation can often be the deciding factor between triumph and defeat. Mental rehearsal techniques stand out as a pivotal tool in your arsenal, allowing you to envision and navigate the myriad scenarios you might encounter during high-pressure competitions. This method is not about daydreaming passively but engaging actively with various competition scenarios in your mind's eye, crafting responses and strategies that you can later execute with confidence.

Think of mental rehearsal as your mental sandbox to build and test your strategies without the physical toll of actual competition. By visualizing different competition scenarios, you're not only familiarizing yourself with potential challenges but also equipping yourself to handle whatever comes your way. For instance, imagine you're a soccer player facing a penalty shootout in a championship game. Through mental rehearsal, you can visualize yourself scoring under different conditions—perhaps with the crowd roaring or, in utter silence, with the game on the line. Each successful visualization reinforces your self-belief and muscle memory, making you more likely to succeed when the moment arrives.

Developing a comprehensive mental game plan is equally crucial. This plan includes detailed strategies for every phase of the competition, tailored to your specific role and responsibilities within the team. It also comprises contingency plans for unexpected situations such as injuries, weather changes, or unforeseen plays from the opposition. To build this, start by analyzing past performances to identify areas of strength and improvement. Engage with your coach to understand the tactical demands of the upcoming competition and align your mental preparation with these strategies. This plan should be a living document, revisited and revised as you gain more insight through training and competition, ensuring it remains aligned with your evolving capabilities and circumstances.

The role of simulation training in preparing for high-stakes competition cannot be overstated. Simulating game-day conditions as closely as possible can provide a physically and mentally enriching rehearsal. This could involve setting up practice sessions that mimic the upcoming competition venue's conditions, complete with similar noise levels and crowd sizes, and even playing at the same time of day as the scheduled event. For team sports, coaches might organize scrimmages that impose game-day tactics both from your team and your upcoming opponents. These simulations help solidify your mental game plan, allowing you to navigate high-pressure situations more smoothly because they feel familiar, reducing the element of surprise and associated stress.

Feedback and adjustment form the final pillar of effective mental preparation. After each competition, take the time to reflect on your performance, particularly noting how well you executed your mental game plan. Discuss with your coach what strategies worked and what didn't, and why. This feedback is crucial for making informed adjustments to your mental preparation strategies, ensuring continuous improvement. It's essential to approach this process with an open mind and a commitment to self-improvement, understanding that the goal is to refine your approach continuously to better meet the challenges of high-stakes competitions.

By integrating these mental preparation strategies into your regular training regimen, you're not just preparing to compete; you're preparing to excel. With each mental rehearsal, each strategic planning session, and each simulated training, you're building a stronger, more resilient mindset that thrives under pressure. This proactive approach to mental preparation enhances your performance during key competitions and instills a greater sense of confidence and control, whatever the competition may bring.

HOW TO CHANNEL NERVOUS ENERGY INTO POSITIVE OUTCOMES

Nervous energy before a big game or performance isn't just common; it's a natural physiological response to what your body perceives as a challenge. This surge of adrenaline can lead to increased heart rate, faster breathing, and heightened alertness. While these responses are intended to prepare you for 'fight or flight' in sports, they need to be finely tuned to work to your advantage rather than lead to overwhelm. Understanding this nervous energy and learning to channel it effectively can transform it from a hindrance to a powerful tool that enhances your athletic performance.

When you feel those familiar butterflies in your stomach or that rush of adrenaline, it's your body gearing up for the demands of competition. If not managed, this nervous energy can lead to tension, quick exhaustion, or mental blocks, which are detrimental when you need to perform your best. However, when redirected correctly, this same energy can increase your alertness, improve your reaction times, and boost your endurance. The key lies in not suppressing this energy but harnessing it through specific techniques that align with your sports performance needs.

One effective method to redirect nervous energy is through intense physical warm-ups. These are not just about stretching muscles but about priming your body and mind for the task ahead. Engage in dynamic warm-ups that mimic the movements of your sport, increasing in intensity to match the surge of adrenaline. For example, if you're a basketball player, this could involve short sprints, high jumps, or agility drills that elevate your heart rate and sharpen your focus. The idea is to match your physical exertion with your internal energy levels so that by the time the game starts, your body and mind are in sync, ready to channel all that nervous energy into the game.

Strategic game planning is another crucial technique in managing nervous energy. This involves going into each game with a clear plan of what you want to achieve and how you intend to handle high-pressure moments. This preparation should be detailed, covering various scenarios you might face during the competition. When you have a plan, your mind has a roadmap to follow, which can help focus nervous energy on execution rather than on the anxiety of what might happen. This clarity can be incredibly calming, directing your mental and physical resources towards goal-oriented actions rather than unproductive worry.

Positive self-talk is an invaluable tool in transforming anxiety into motivation and confidence. This involves actively replacing negative thoughts that arise from nervous energy with affirmations that reinforce your abilities and readiness. Phrases like "I am prepared," "I can handle this," or "I am here to perform my best" are not just motivational; they reprogram your mind to view the competition as an opportunity to excel rather than a threat. This shift in perspective can significantly alter your emotional and physiological response to stress, turning nervous energy into a motivational surge that drives you to perform with confidence.

To illustrate the real-world application of these techniques, consider the case of a collegiate volleyball player known for her powerful serves but who struggled with game-day anxiety. By integrating intense targeted warm-ups into her pre-game routine, she was able to align her physical state with her mental arousal, using the adrenaline to enhance her serve speed and accuracy. Additionally, strategic game planning helped her focus on executing well-practiced plays rather than worrying about the scoreboard. Her coaches also worked with her on positive self-talk, helping transform her pre-game nerves into a focused determination to excel. This comprehensive approach allowed her to use her nervous energy to fuel her performance rather than detract from it, leading to notable improvements in her game-day executions.

These strategies, when practiced regularly, can help you master the art of channeling nervous energy effectively. By embracing and redirecting this energy, you enhance your performance and develop greater mental toughness and resilience, invaluable qualities both on and off the field.

LONG-TERM STRATEGIES FOR MANAGING STRESS IN YOUNG ATHLETES

Adjusting your lifestyle to manage stress effectively is not just about making temporary changes during competitions; it's about embedding healthy habits into your daily routine that bolster your mental and physical resilience over the long term. Regular physical activity, which is already a part of any athlete's life, should be complemented with activities that help in stress reduction and recovery, such as yoga or swimming. These activities not only provide physical relief but also improve mental well-being by reducing symptoms of anxiety and depression.

Nutrition also plays a crucial role in managing stress. Eating a balanced diet rich in fruits, vegetables, lean proteins, and whole grains can provide the necessary nutrients that the body needs to cope with stress. Omega-3 fatty acids, found in fish like salmon and in flaxseeds, are particularly effective in reducing the symptoms of stress and anxiety. Ensuring that your body has the right fuel can help stabilize your mood, improve your sleep patterns, and enhance your overall resilience to stress.

Sufficient sleep is another pillar of effective stress management. Athletes may need more sleep than the average person due to the physical demands placed on their bodies. Lack of sleep not only impairs physical performance but also increases susceptibility to stress. Establishing a regular sleep schedule that includes 7-9 hours of quality sleep per night can drastically improve your ability to manage stress. Techniques such as limiting screen time before bed, using relaxation exercises, or maintaining a comfortable sleep environment can aid in achieving deep, restorative sleep.

Social support from family, friends, and teammates plays a vital role in managing long-term stress. Being part of a supportive social network can provide emotional comfort and practical help during tough times. Teammates, who often understand the specific pressures associated with sports, can be particularly valuable in providing support. They can offer motivation, help in developing coping strategies, and sometimes just be there to listen. Family and friends provide a broader support network that helps keep everything in perspective, reminding you that there is life beyond sport, which can be vital in reducing sports-related stress.

Continuous mental skills training is essential for maintaining and enhancing your mental toughness. Techniques such as mindfulness, meditation, and cognitive-behavioral strategies should be incorporated into your regular training regimen, not just used in the lead-up to competitions. Regular practice of these techniques can help modify your response to stress, making you less reactive and more proactive in managing stressors. This kind of training strengthens your mental resilience, allowing you to handle the ups and downs of competitive sports with greater ease.

Seeking professional help is a step that should be normalized in sports culture. Just as you would see a physical therapist for an injury, consulting a psychologist for mental struggles should be considered an integral part of your health care. Athletes might feel overwhelmed by stress or anxiety that seems unmanageable through usual coping strategies. In such cases, professionals can provide personalized guidance and treatment plans that address your specific needs, helping you maintain your mental health and perform your best.

In this chapter, we've explored various strategies to manage stress and anxiety, focusing on long-term solutions that build resilience and improve your overall well-being. From lifestyle adjustments like balanced nutrition and sufficient sleep to the importance of a supportive social network and continuous mental skills training, these strategies are designed to equip you with the tools you need to handle the pressures of sports. Seeking professional help has also been emphasized as a critical component of managing overwhelming stress. As we move forward, remember that managing stress and anxiety is not just about coping with the pressures of the moment; it's about building a foundation of mental toughness that will support your athletic and personal growth for years to come. In the next chapter, we will delve into building and sustaining confidence, a key aspect of mental toughness that complements the strategies discussed here.

CHAPTER 4
BUILDING AND SUSTAINING CONFIDENCE

"Believe you can and you're halfway there."
— Theodore Roosevelt

CONFIDENCE CAN BE the fuel that powers you through the finish line or the anchor that drags you down before you even start. As a young athlete, the cultivation of a solid, unwavering confidence is not just beneficial; it's essential. This chapter delves into the transformative potential of positive self-talk, a tool that can elevate your performance and help you navigate the turbulent waters of competitive sports with poise and resilience.

THE POWER OF POSITIVE SELF-TALK IN SPORTS

Introduce Positive Self-Talk

Imagine you're at the starting line of a race, surrounded by competitors who seem just as prepared, if not more. What goes through your mind in that critical moment can significantly influence your performance. This is where positive self-talk, a powerful mental strategy, comes into play. Positive self-talk involves consciously generating affirmative statements to yourself, which can help shift your mindset from doubt and fear to confidence and focus. It's about replacing thoughts like "I can't do this" with "I am prepared, and I will give my best." This technique isn't about denying reality but about reshaping it to serve you better, transforming your inner dialogue into a supportive, encouraging voice.

TECHNIQUES FOR DEVELOPING POSITIVE SELF-TALK

Developing effective positive self-talk requires practice and intentionality. Start by becoming more aware of your negative self-talk. During training or competitions, catch yourself when you think negatively and consciously choose to replace those thoughts with positive affirmations. For instance, if you miss a shot or lose a point, instead of thinking, "I always mess up," tell yourself, "I can learn from this mistake."

Create a list of personalized affirmations that resonate with your sports goals and challenges. These might include phrases like "I am strong," "I improve with every practice," or "I thrive under pressure." Rehearse these affirmations regularly, not just during your sport but throughout your day. The more familiar these thoughts become, the more naturally they will arise when you need them most.

ROLE IN OVERCOMING CHALLENGES

Positive self-talk is particularly effective in helping athletes manage and overcome common sports challenges. Performance anxiety, for instance, can be alleviated by affirmations that focus on preparedness and past successes, reminding you of your capabilities and resilience. During critical moments in a competition, having the ability to pull from a reserve of positive, affirming thoughts can be the difference between faltering and flourishing.

For example, consider a tennis player facing match point in a crucial game. The pressure is immense, with every stroke carrying weight. By engaging in positive self-talk, the athlete maintains focus and composure, telling themselves, "I have practiced for this moment, I am ready, and I can handle this," effectively channeling their nervous energy into focused action.

PRACTICE SCENARIOS

To integrate positive self-talk into your routine, consider these practice scenarios:

- **During Difficult Practices:** When the training gets tough and you feel like giving up, engage in positive self-talk by reminding yourself of the purpose and goals of your efforts. "Each step makes me faster" or "This pain is temporary, but the improvement is lasting" can keep you motivated.
- **After Errors or Mistakes:** It's easy to be hard on yourself after a mistake, but this is the perfect time to practice self-compassion and resilience through positive self-talk. "Mistakes are part of learning, and I am improving every day" can help you move past errors more quickly.
- **When Facing Stronger Opponents:** Instead of being intimidated, use positive self-talk to boost your courage and determination. Phrases like "I am here because I deserve to be" and "I can learn from this challenge" can transform anxiety into excitement and motivation.

By embracing positive self-talk, you're not just improving your sports performance; you're also setting the foundation for a more confident and resilient mindset in all areas of life. As you continue to develop this skill, you'll find that the benefits extend far beyond the playing field, enhancing your interactions and achievements in academics, personal relationships, and future career endeavors. The power of your thoughts cannot be underestimated—it's time to make them your allies in the quest for success and personal fulfillment in sports and beyond.

OVERCOMING SELF-DOUBT AFTER SETBACKS

Setbacks and failures, while often seen as obstacles, are inherent parts of growth in any athlete's journey. However, the shadow of self-doubt that can follow a setback has the potential to cloud your vision and derail your progress if not appropriately addressed. Recognizing and managing self-doubt is, therefore, crucial, not just for your performance but for your overall mental health. Self-doubt usually manifests as an internal voice that undercuts your confidence, questions your skills, and magnifies your fears, making it essential to identify these thoughts early and counteract them effectively.

The first step in combating self-doubt is to recognize its signs. These might include hesitancy in making decisions, a tendency to overanalyze your performance, or a pattern of focusing only on what went wrong rather than what was achieved. Understanding that these thoughts are a natural response to disappointment can help you begin to address them. It's important to acknowledge your feelings without letting them define your capabilities or future potential. This acknowledgment can empower you to take proactive steps toward rebuilding your confidence.

Reframing negative thoughts is a powerful strategy to combat self-doubt. This involves consciously shifting your perspective on the thoughts that fuel doubt. For example, instead of thinking, "I always mess up under pressure," you could reframe this to, "Every moment of pressure is an opportunity to improve my focus and execution." This shift doesn't dismiss the reality of your experience but changes the narrative from one of perpetual failure to one of growth and potential. Focusing on the effort you're putting in rather than just the outcomes helps as well. This means valuing your hard work, dedication, and perseverance, regardless of the immediate results. Such a focus reinforces the understanding that progress in sports is often non-linear and that persistence is key.

Setting realistic expectations is another vital part of overcoming self-doubt. These expectations should stretch your abilities but remain achievable. Unrealistic goals can feed into self-doubt by creating a gap between your expectations and your performance. Work with coaches to set achievable targets that align with your current skills and future potential. Achieving these can provide a significant confidence boost, which in turn can diminish self-doubt.

Reflective practices like journaling or discussions with coaches can also be incredibly beneficial. They provide a structured way to analyze your performances, identify patterns in your thoughts and behaviors, and develop strategies for improvement. For instance, maintaining a performance journal where you not only record the outcomes but also how you felt, what you did well, and what could be improved can help you see your growth over time. This can be particularly encouraging during times when progress seems slow or invisible.

Beyond personal reflection, hearing about or studying other athletes who have successfully navigated significant setbacks can serve as a potent reminder that recovery and success are possible. Consider the story of a professional athlete who experienced a major injury mid-season and faced a long recovery period filled with doubt about returning to their previous physical ability. Through a dedicated recovery and rehab regimen, strategic goal-setting, and mental conditioning focused on positive self-talk and visualization, this athlete not only returned to their sport but also went on to achieve new personal bests. Stories like these underscore the importance of resilience and strategic recovery, providing practical examples and emotional inspiration to athletes facing similar challenges.

As you continue to navigate your athletic career, remember that self-doubt does not have to be a permanent roadblock. With the right strategies and support, you can transform setbacks into stepping stones for success, using them to build a stronger, more resilient approach to your sport and life. These practices help overcome self-doubt and contribute to a deeper, more enduring sense of self-confidence, equipping you with the mental tools to face future challenges with a proactive and positive mindset.

HOW ROLE MODELS CAN INFLUENCE YOUNG ATHLETES' CONFIDENCE

When you, as a young athlete, think about the sports figures you admire most, it's often their achievements, resilience, and character that stand out. These role models, whether elite athletes or local coaches, play a pivotal role in shaping your aspirations and attitudes toward your own athletic career. Choosing the right role models is more than just picking a favorite athlete; it involves identifying individuals who exemplify the values and traits you wish to embody both on and off the field.

When selecting role models, it's important to look beyond just their success or statistics. Consider their journey, the challenges they've overcome, their work ethic, and how they handle both victories and defeats. Positive role models demonstrate resilience in the face of setbacks and maintain a humble demeanor in success, which can inspire you to adopt a similar mindset. Also, consider the ways these individuals contribute to their community, interact with fans, and handle their critics. Athletes who engage in community service or take the time to mentor younger athletes show that being a great athlete isn't just about performance; it's also about character and impact.

Learning from your role models can be transformative. Observing how your role models train, handle pressure, rebound from poor performances, and conduct themselves publicly provides a blueprint for professional and personal growth. For instance, if your role model is known for their meticulous preparation before games, integrate similar routines into your schedule and notice how it affects your confidence and performance. If they are vocal about their goals and the steps they are taking to achieve them, use this as motivation to set clear, actionable goals for yourself. This type of modeling can significantly boost your confidence as you begin to see real improvements in your performance that mirror those of your role models.

The impact of seeing someone similar to yourself succeed cannot be overstated. It reinforces the belief that your goals are attainable and that the hurdles you face can be overcome. This can be particularly powerful for young athletes from underrepresented backgrounds.

Seeing someone of the same gender, race, or community achieving great things in sports can inspire a deep sense of possibility and pride. This connection boosts self-esteem and motivates you to pursue your ambitions with renewed vigor and optimism.

INTERACTIVE ACTIVITIES

To actively engage with the concept of role modeling, consider participating in interactive activities that bring you closer to the athletes you admire. Interviews, whether reading them or conducting them if possible, are excellent ways to gain deeper insights into the minds of successful athletes. These interactions can reveal the nuances of their mental and physical preparation, offering valuable lessons that you can apply to your training and competitions.

Engaging in role model research projects is another enriching activity. This could involve preparing a presentation, project, or report on the career of a role model, analyzing their performance data, and understanding the factors contributing to their success and longevity in sports. Such projects deepen your understanding and improve your analytical skills, which are crucial both on and off the field.

Attending live games to observe your role models in action offers a firsthand look at their skills and behaviors in real time. Pay attention to how they communicate with teammates, handle stress during the game, and their strategies for maintaining focus under pressure. Observing these details can provide practical strategies that you can emulate in your sports endeavors.

By incorporating these interactive activities into your routine, you not only stay inspired but also gain practical skills and knowledge that bolster your growth as an athlete. Watching, learning, and interacting with your role models provides a continuous source of motivation and learning, helping you to refine your abilities and approach to sports with a more informed and inspired perspective. As you continue to develop your skills and build your confidence, remember the influential power of positive role models and strive to emulate not only their successes but also their resilience, work ethic, and commitment to excellence.

THE IMPACT OF PEER SUPPORT IN BUILDING TEAM CONFIDENCE

In the dynamic world of sports, the support of peers—your teammates—plays an indispensable role in shaping the atmosphere of your team and significantly influencing individual and collective performance. Peer support in this context refers to the encouragement, advice, and camaraderie shared among team members. This supportive network is essential not only for the psychological welfare of the athletes but also for fostering a team environment conducive to success. When teammates support each other, the trust and bonds formed can transform a group of individuals into a unified entity with a shared vision of victory and excellence.

To cultivate a robust system of peer support, it's crucial to implement techniques that encourage strong relationships among team members. Team-building exercises are more than just fun or productive activities; they are strategic tools designed to enhance communication, build trust, and promote understanding among athletes. For instance, activities that require teamwork and problem-solving can improve cohesion and help athletes appreciate each other's strengths and weaknesses. These might include outdoor team sports, problem-solving challenges, or trust-building exercises.

Peer mentoring programs are another effective avenue for strengthening team dynamics. Pairing experienced team members with newer or younger athletes can facilitate a mentorship dynamic that helps newer athletes acclimate to the team's culture and expectations while providing leadership opportunities for veteran team members. This helps transfer knowledge and experience and creates a sense of responsibility and pride among the mentors, which can significantly boost their confidence and investment in the team's success.

Cooperative training sessions, where athletes are encouraged to work together toward common goals, also play a critical role in enhancing peer support. These sessions could involve group workouts, relay practices, or team challenges that require athletes to support each other's efforts. Such activities improve physical conditioning and reinforce the ethos of mutual support and collective effort.

Open communication about successes and struggles is vital in cultivating a supportive team environment. Encouraging athletes to share their achievements fosters a culture of celebration and mutual joy, which can be incredibly motivating. Similarly, creating a safe space for athletes to express their challenges or concerns can foster empathy and support within the team. This openness helps build a supportive network where athletes feel valued and understood, significantly boosting team morale and individual confidence.

One illustrative case of successful peer support involves a high school basketball team that was struggling with internal conflicts and poor performance. The coach introduced regular team-building retreats, established a peer mentorship program, and restructured training to include more cooperative activities. Over the season, these initiatives transformed the team dynamics. Players began to communicate more openly, trust in each other's abilities strengthened, and the overall morale improved. The team's performance enhanced remarkably, culminating in a winning streak that led them to the state championships. This turnaround underscored the power of peer support in overcoming obstacles and achieving success.

In another example, a collegiate soccer team faced a series of defeats that left the team disheartened and in disarray. The coach facilitated workshops where players could openly discuss their feelings about the games, their performance, and their interactions with teammates. These sessions helped clear misunderstandings, align goals, and restore trust among the team members. Following these interventions, the team experienced a renewed sense of unity and purpose, which was reflected in their improved coordination on the field and a better overall performance in subsequent matches.

These cases highlight how fostering a supportive peer environment can be transformative for sports teams. By focusing on building and nurturing these relationships, teams can create a resilient and encouraging environment that enhances the confidence and performance of all members. As you continue to engage in or lead sports teams, remember the strength that lies in unity and mutual support. Peer support is not just about building a better team but also about crafting a community within the team that stands strong together in the face of challenges and celebrates together in the joy of achievements.

CELEBRATING SMALL WINS: A KEY TO SUSTAINED CONFIDENCE

In the relentless pursuit of excellence in sports, it's easy to overlook the smaller milestones, focusing only on the ultimate goals. However, recognizing and celebrating small victories is essential for building and sustaining confidence throughout your athletic career. Small wins, whether improving a personal time, mastering a new technique, or simply completing a challenging workout, all contribute to a sense of progress and achievement. Though seemingly minor, these moments are the building blocks of major successes, providing a steady stream of motivation and a tangible sense of advancement.

The process of celebrating these small wins starts with recognizing them. As an athlete, you're often your own harshest critic, which can sometimes obscure your view of the progress you're making. To counter this, develop a habit of identifying and acknowledging every improvement, no matter how small. This could be as simple as completing a set number of practices in a week, increasing the weights during your workout, or improving your reaction time. Each of these achievements is a step forward and deserves recognition.

Tracking these improvements can be effectively managed through various methods such as performance journals, progress charts, or digital apps specifically designed for athletes. A performance journal, for example, allows you to document not only your physical performance metrics but also your mental and emotional state, providing a holistic view of your progress. This can be particularly uplifting on days when you feel like you haven't made much progress, as looking back over your journal can show you just how far you've come. Progress charts are another helpful tool, offering a visual representation of your improvements over time, which can be incredibly satisfying and motivating. Digital apps can provide a more tech-savvy approach, offering features like goal-setting, reminders, motivational quotes, and tracking your progress in real-time.

The psychological benefits of celebrating these wins are substantial. Each small victory enhances your self-esteem, reinforcing your belief in your abilities. This boost in self-confidence is crucial, especially after setbacks or during plateaus in your training where visible progress might slow down. Furthermore, the act of celebrating these achievements can reinforce positive behaviors, encouraging you to continue putting in the effort required to achieve your long-term goals. This creates a positive feedback loop, where each small success fuels the next, keeping you engaged and focused on your developmental journey.

Encouraging continuous improvement through the celebration of small wins is about creating a mindset that values progress over perfection. This perspective helps you stay committed to your goals and keeps you motivated, even when the path becomes challenging. It's about understanding that improvement in sports isn't always linear and that perseverance through the ups and downs is what leads to success. Celebrating these wins, therefore, isn't just about acknowledging your achievements; it's about setting the stage for future successes, maintaining a positive and growth-oriented mindset, and continuously pushing the boundaries of your capabilities.

As you integrate these practices into your routine, remember that the journey to the top is composed of many small steps. Each step, no matter how small, is a reason to celebrate because it represents forward movement in your athletic and personal growth. This approach not only enhances your enjoyment of the sport but also builds a resilient and confident athlete, ready to take on any challenge with a positive and determined spirit.

As this chapter closes, reflect on the power of small victories and their role in building a strong, confident foundation for your athletic career. Embrace each achievement, learn from every challenge, and continue to strive for excellence, knowing that every step forward is a step toward achieving your ultimate goals. Up next, we will explore how cultivating resilience and grit not only complements the confidence you've built but also prepares you for the inevitable challenges that lie ahead in your athletic pursuits. Rest assured, the skills and mindsets you are developing are shaping you into a better athlete and a formidable competitor in all areas of life.

CHAPTER 5
CULTIVATING RESILIENCE AND GRIT

"Success is not final, failure is not fatal: It is the courage to continue that counts."
– Winston Churchill

IMAGINE you are in the final seconds of a crucial game. The score is tied, and the ball is in your hands. You take the shot, and... you miss. The game goes to overtime, and your team eventually loses. In these moments, your heart sinks, your spirit dampens, and self-doubt may start creeping in. Yet, it is precisely in these moments that the seeds of resilience and grit are sown. This chapter is about transforming failure from a source of pain to a pillar of strength, a fundamental shift that can redefine your athletic journey.

UNDERSTANDING THE ROLE OF FAILURE IN ATHLETIC DEVELOPMENT

Reframe Failure as Opportunity

In sports, as in life, failure is inevitable. However, how you interpret and respond to these failures can make all the difference. Viewing failure as an opportunity rather than a setback is crucial. This mindset shift allows you to embrace each misstep as a learning moment, a chance to delve deeper into your performance and extract valuable insights. Think of each game not just as a potential win or loss but as a stepping stone towards your personal and athletic growth.

When you start seeing failure as a necessary part of learning, your approach to training and competing changes. You become more willing to take risks and push your boundaries because you know that even if the outcome is not what you hoped, there will be valuable lessons to take away. This approach not only enhances your skills but also builds mental toughness, preparing you for higher levels of competition.

PSYCHOLOGICAL IMPACT OF FAILURE

The psychological impact of failure can be profound, but managing this impact effectively is key to turning painful experiences into productive ones. Initially, failure can trigger feelings of disappointment, anger, or frustration. However, by adopting a reflective approach, you can start to analyze these emotions and understand their origins. Ask yourself what about the failure triggered these feelings. Was it the missed opportunity, the reaction of your teammates, or the pressure of expectations?

Understanding these emotional triggers allows you to address them directly, perhaps by adjusting your expectations, improving communication with your teammates, or modifying your preparation for games. This reflective process alleviates the emotional weight of failure and equips you with emotional resilience, turning emotional insights into actionable improvements.

EDUCATIONAL VALUE OF MISTAKES

Mistakes are not just missteps; they are the curriculum in the school of improvement. Each error provides a unique insight into your performance and strategic thinking. For example, a missed shot in basketball can reveal several learning opportunities—perhaps it highlights a need for better technique, better decision-making under pressure, or even physical conditioning. By analyzing these moments carefully, you and your coach can tailor your training to address these specific areas, turning weaknesses into strengths over time.

Encouraging a culture of reflection and openness about mistakes within your team can multiply these benefits. When teammates share their experiences and insights from failures, it creates a rich learning environment where everyone can benefit from each other's experiences, accelerating collective and individual improvement.

ENCOURAGE A CULTURE OF EXPERIMENTATION

Cultivating a team culture that values experimentation and learning from mistakes is crucial. In such an environment, athletes are encouraged to try new strategies and techniques during training and games. This experimental approach should be supported by a coaching philosophy that values long-term development over short-term results. For example, a coach might encourage a soccer player to try different shooting techniques in various game scenarios to find what works best under pressure.

This culture of experimentation should be seen as an integral part of development, where failures are not just tolerated but are viewed as essential steps in the learning process. It promotes creativity and innovation in strategies and techniques, which can lead to significant improvements in team performance and individual skills.

Encouraging this mindset requires consistent communication from coaches and team leaders, reinforcing the message that the team values growth and learning above all. Celebrating innovative attempts and constructive risk-taking, even when they don't always lead to success, can reinforce this culture, making athletes more resilient and adaptive in competitive situations.

You can build a foundation of resilience and grit by embracing failure as a learning tool, managing the emotional aftermath of setbacks, and fostering an environment that encourages risk-taking and reflection. This approach not only enhances your performance but also prepares you for the challenges of competitive sports, ensuring that each step back is followed by two steps forward.

STRATEGIES FOR BOUNCING BACK AFTER A LOSS

When the final whistle blows, and the scoreboard isn't in your favor, the weight of loss can feel overwhelming. It's natural to feel disappointed, but how you respond in these moments can define your future as much as any victory. Dealing with loss is a crucial skill, one that involves immediate strategies to manage the initial emotional impact and long-term techniques to build resilience for future challenges.

IMMEDIATE POST-LOSS STRATEGIES

Right after a loss, the emotional landscape can be difficult to navigate. Engaging in constructive self-talk is your first tool for recovery. Remind yourself that this loss, like every part of your athletic experience, is a chance to learn and grow. Shift your internal dialogue from criticism to encouragement. Replace thoughts like "I failed" with "I can learn from this." This reframing can help prevent a single defeat from damaging your self-esteem and motivation.

Controlled breathing is another powerful technique that you can use right after a game to regain composure and mitigate the physical symptoms of stress and disappointment. Try the 4-7-8 breathing technique: breathe in deeply for 4 seconds, hold your breath for 7 seconds, and exhale slowly for 8 seconds. Repeat this sequence a few times to help calm your nervous system and clear your mind, making you better equipped to handle the emotional aftermath of the game.

Additionally, debriefing with your coach can be incredibly beneficial. This should be more than just a review of what went wrong; it's a supportive dialogue that helps you understand the loss within the broader context of your development. Your coach can help you identify specific areas for improvement and highlight aspects of your performance that were successful, which can be easily overlooked in the heat of the moment. This balanced feedback helps you build a realistic perspective on your performance, emphasizing learning and growth over criticism.

LONG-TERM RESILIENCE BUILDING

Building resilience is a long-term process that involves regularly engaging in practices that strengthen your mental and emotional endurance. Routine stress-reduction practices such as yoga, meditation, or even simple daily mindfulness exercises can significantly enhance your ability to handle the pressures of competitive sports. These practices help cultivate a sense of calm and control, which are invaluable during high-stress situations in games or tournaments.

Another aspect of building long-term resilience is actively working on your emotional endurance. This involves setting challenges for yourself in training and less critical competitions to develop your ability to persist under pressure. Over time, these challenges help you build a mental "toughness reserve" that you can draw on during more significant competitions. It's about gradually increasing your capacity to handle stress and disappointment, so you're better prepared when faced with high-stake situations.

ROLE OF SUPPORT SYSTEMS

Your support system plays a crucial role in helping you bounce back from losses. This network, which may include family, friends, teammates, and coaches, provides emotional comfort and practical advice when you're dealing with disappointment. Openly sharing your feelings with trusted individuals can help alleviate the burden of loss, providing you with different perspectives and emotional support that can reframe your experience.

Teammates, in particular, can relate to your experience directly as they're likely going through the same emotions. Together, you can support each other in processing the loss and finding ways to move forward. This collective resilience not only strengthens team bonds but also fosters a supportive environment where all members feel valued and understood, boosting overall team morale and individual confidence.

LEARNING FROM LOSS

Finally, learning from each loss is one of the most effective long-term strategies for dealing with defeat. This involves a detailed analysis of your performance to identify both strengths and areas for improvement. Discuss these with your coach, and use video replays if possible, to get a clear picture of your gameplay. Focus on specific moments in the game that could have changed the outcome and explore different strategies you might employ in the future.

Document these insights in a performance journal, noting what you've learned and how you plan to apply these lessons in future competitions. This helps turn a negative experience into a positive learning opportunity and tracks your growth over time, providing a tangible record of your development as an athlete. By consistently learning from each loss, you transform these experiences into stepping stones towards success, gradually building a comprehensive toolkit of skills and strategies that enhance your performance and resilience.

DEVELOPING A GROWTH MINDSET IN SPORTS

In competitive sports, the distinction between a growth mindset and a fixed mindset can fundamentally influence an athlete's approach to training, performance, and overall development. A growth mindset, as conceptualized by psychologist Carol Dweck, is characterized by the belief that abilities and intelligence can be developed through dedication, hard work, and a willingness to learn from mistakes. For athletes, embracing a growth mindset means viewing each practice, game, and season as opportunities to enhance skills, deepen understanding, and push beyond current limits.

The importance of a growth mindset in sports cannot be overstressed. It fosters resilience, encourages continuous improvement, and helps athletes bounce back from setbacks with a stronger, more determined resolve. Unlike a fixed mindset, which can stifle progress and resilience by promoting a belief that abilities are static and unchangeable, a growth mindset catalyzes personal development and innovation. Athletes with a growth mindset are more likely to embrace challenges, persist in the face of difficulties, and achieve higher levels of success over time.

Contrasting these two mindsets highlights their impact on an athlete's behavior and performance. Athletes with a fixed mindset may avoid challenges, give up easily, and see effort as fruitless when they don't win. They might feel threatened by the success of others and often attribute setbacks to a lack of inherent ability, which they believe they can do little to change. On the other hand, those with a growth mindset view challenges as essential for growth, persist through difficulties, learn from criticism, and find lessons and inspiration in the success of others. This mindset not only enhances their performance but also contributes to a more fulfilling athletic experience.

To cultivate a growth mindset, start by focusing on effort rather than results. This shift in focus can dramatically change your perception of success. For instance, instead of getting discouraged after a loss, evaluate the effort you put into the game. Reflect on what you did well and identify specific areas where you can improve. This approach not only builds resilience but also aligns with the fundamental principle of a growth mindset: that each effort is a step toward mastering your sport.

Embracing challenges is another critical step in developing a growth mindset. Challenges push you out of your comfort zone and provide the richest opportunities for growth. When faced with a tough opponent or a skill that is difficult to master, instead of backing down, lean into the discomfort. Use it as a fuel to enhance your skills. Each challenge you overcome not only improves your abilities but also reinforces your belief in your capacity to develop and succeed.

The impact of a growth mindset extends beyond training into actual performance. Athletes who embrace this mindset approach competitions as opportunities to apply what they have learned, test their skills, and continue to improve. They are more adaptable and able to respond to the dynamic nature of sports with flexibility and innovation. Moreover, their continuous pursuit of learning and development often leads to better strategies, enhanced techniques, and, ultimately, superior performance.

Developing a growth mindset in sports involves a fundamental shift in how you view your abilities and approach your athletic development. By focusing on effort, embracing challenges, and viewing setbacks as learning opportunities, you can foster a mindset that not only enhances your performance but also drives continual personal growth. This mindset is not just about achieving success in sports; it's about setting a foundation for lifelong learning and achievement, transforming the way you approach challenges on and off the field. As you continue to train and compete, keep this perspective at the forefront of your mind, and watch as it transforms your approach to sports and life.

STORIES OF RESILIENCE: HOW YOUNG ATHLETES OVERCAME ADVERSITY

Resilience is not just a buzzword; it's a critical attribute that can define the trajectory of an athlete's career. It's about bouncing back from setbacks with a stronger, more determined spirit. This resilience can often be best understood through the stories of young athletes who faced considerable adversities yet emerged victorious, not just in terms of their sport but also in terms of their personal growth.

Take, for instance, the story of a young gymnast named Emily. At the age of 15, Emily suffered a severe injury during a routine training session, which doctors said could potentially end her gymnastics career. Instead of succumbing to despair, Emily approached her recovery with an unwavering resolve. Her rehabilitation was not just physical but also mental; she engaged in visualization exercises, picturing herself performing routines with precision and grace. Over months of physical therapy and mental conditioning, not only did Emily recover, but she also returned to the sport with a new level of passion and proficiency. She went on to win a national championship, a testament to her resilience and determination. From Emily's journey, young athletes can learn the importance of perseverance and the power of a positive mindset in overcoming physical setbacks.

Another inspiring story comes from a high school basketball player named Marcus. During his sophomore year, Marcus's team lost in the first round of a regional tournament, a game that many expected them to win easily. The loss was a significant emotional blow to the team, but Marcus used it as fuel to improve. He spent the off-season refining his skills, studying game films, improving his physical conditioning, and mentoring younger players on his team. His leadership and improved gameplay were pivotal in leading his team to a state championship the following year. Marcus's story highlights not just the importance of resilience in the face of defeat but also the role of leadership and mentorship in fostering a team's collective resilience.

These stories are not just narratives; they are powerful lessons in emotional management and adaptive problem-solving. They teach that setbacks can be transformed into opportunities for growth and that resilience can be cultivated through deliberate practice and a positive outlook.

For those looking to draw continuous inspiration from such stories, watching video interviews or documentaries about athletes who demonstrate remarkable resilience can be incredibly beneficial. These real-life examples provide not only inspiration but also practical strategies that can be adopted.

By exploring different athlete stories, young athletes can find role models who exemplify the essence of resilience, providing tangible examples to emulate. These athletes' journeys underscore the importance of maintaining focus on long-term goals, staying positive in the face of challenges, and continuously striving for personal and professional growth. Whether it's through their dedication, innovative problem-solving, or emotional strength, these stories offer invaluable lessons that extend well beyond the sports arena, equipping young athletes with the mindset to thrive in all areas of life.

CREATING A PERSONAL RESILIENCE PLAN

Developing a personal resilience plan is vital to mapping out a strategy for success, not just in sports but in handling the challenges life throws at you. This plan isn't about preparing for specific obstacles but rather about creating a robust framework that allows you to thrive in the face of adversity. To begin crafting your resilience plan, start with setting clear, attainable resilience goals. These should be specific objectives that enhance your mental toughness, such as improving your ability to stay calm under pressure during games or enhancing your capacity to recover from setbacks more swiftly.

Identify potential obstacles that might impede these goals. This might involve recognizing personal triggers that cause stress or anxiety or external factors like a challenging competitive schedule. Awareness of these hurdles is crucial as it allows you to devise specific strategies to overcome them. For instance, if one of your goals is to maintain calm during critical game moments, a potential obstacle might be the intense pressure and noise from spectators. Preparing for this, you could integrate simulated crowd noise during practice sessions, gradually increasing the volume as you become more accustomed to the distraction.

Incorporating routine resilience practices into your daily or weekly schedule is essential. Daily mindfulness exercises can enhance your mental clarity and focus, while reflective journaling can offer deeper insights into your emotional responses and coping mechanisms during both training and competitions. Scenario planning is also beneficial; regularly visualize different game situations, focusing on how you would respond to various challenges. These practices build resilience and make these responses more intuitive, enhancing your performance when it counts.

Feedback plays a critical role in the effectiveness of your resilience plan. Regular input from coaches and peers can provide you with an external perspective on your progress. This feedback should be constructive, focusing on areas of improvement and reinforcing what you're doing well. It's important to be open to this feedback, viewing it as an essential element of your growth. Adjust your plan based on this feedback, fine-tuning your strategies and practices to better align with your goals.

Regular review and adjustment of your resilience plan are necessary to ensure it remains relevant and effective as you grow and face new challenges. This might mean setting new goals as you achieve your current ones or modifying your strategies in response to changing circumstances in your sport or personal life. This dynamic approach ensures that your resilience plan evolves with you, continuously supporting your development as an athlete and an individual.

This ongoing process of planning, executing, receiving feedback, and adjusting forms a cycle of continual improvement. By consistently applying yourself to this cycle, you enhance your resilience and empower yourself with the confidence and skills necessary to face any challenge. Remember, resilience isn't a static trait but a dynamic skill that you can develop and strengthen over time. Through deliberate practice and commitment, your personal resilience plan will not only prepare you for the demands of your sport but also equip you with the mental tools necessary for life's unpredictable challenges.

As this chapter closes, reflect on the structured approach to building resilience that has been outlined. From identifying and setting specific resilience goals to incorporating routine practices and seeking valuable feedback, each step is designed to foster a robust and adaptable mindset. This chapter has set the stage for you, providing the tools and strategies necessary to cultivate resilience and grit. As you move forward, carry these lessons with you, applying them not only in your athletic endeavors but in every aspect of your life where resilience is required. The journey towards building a resilient mindset is ongoing.

With each step, you grow stronger and more prepared for whatever lies ahead.

In the next chapter, we will explore balancing athletics with life, an essential aspect of maintaining overall well-being and ensuring that your sports commitments enhance, rather than detract from, your life experiences.

MAKE A DIFFERENCE WITH YOUR REVIEW

UNLOCK THE POWER OF GENEROSITY

"Helping one person might not change the whole world, but it could change the world for one person."

People who give without expectation live longer, happier lives and make more money. So if we've got a shot at that during our time together, darn it, I'm going to try.

To make that happen, I have a question for you...

Would you help someone you've never met, even if you never got credit for it?

Who is this person you ask? They are like you. Or, at least, like you used to be. Less experienced, wanting to make a difference, and needing help, but not sure where to look.

Our mission is to make *Mental Toughness for Young Athletes Unleashed* accessible to everyone. Everything we do stems from that mission. And, the only way for us to accomplish that mission is by reaching...well...everyone.

This is where you come in. Most people do, in fact, judge a book by its cover (and its reviews). So here's my ask on behalf of a struggling young athlete you've never met:

Please help other young athletes by leaving this book a review.

Your gift costs no money and takes less than 60 seconds to make real, but it can change a fellow young athlete's life forever. Your review could help...

- ...one more young athlete find their inner strength.
- ...one more coach inspire their team.
- ...one more parent support their child's dreams.
- ...one more dream come true.

To get that 'feel good' feeling and help this person for real, all you have to do is...and it takes less than 60 seconds... leave a review.

Simply scan the QR code below to leave your review:

If you feel good about helping another young athlete, you are my kind of person. Welcome to the club. You're one of us.

I'm that much more excited to help you boost focus, resilience, and confidence and improve your performance faster than you can possibly imagine. You'll love the strategies I'm about to share in the coming chapters.

Thank you from the bottom of my heart. Now, back to our regularly scheduled programming.

- Your biggest fan, Rush Hemphill

PS - Fun fact: If you provide something of value to another person, it makes you more valuable to them. If you'd like goodwill straight from another young athlete - and you believe this book will help them - send this book their way.

CHAPTER 6
BALANCING ATHLETICS WITH LIFE

"You can't put a limit on anything. The more you dream, the farther you get."
— Michael Phelps

IMAGINE YOU ARE WALKING A TIGHTROPE, carefully balancing your steps to maintain balance and equilibrium. Now, replace that tightrope with the demands of your athletic and academic commitments—this is the daily reality for student-athletes like you. Mastering this balance is not just about preventing a fall; it's about moving forward confidently, maximizing both your sports performance and academic achievements. This chapter dives deep into effective and practical strategies for managing your time, a fundamental skill that supports your dual ambitions and enhances your overall life quality.

EFFECTIVE TIME MANAGEMENT FOR STUDENT-ATHLETES

Introduce Time Management Tools

In the digital age, the traditional notebook and pen have been supplemented with innovative tools designed to streamline your busy schedule. As a student-athlete, leveraging technology through calendars, apps, and digital planners can transform how you organize your day, week, and season. Tools like Google Calendar, Todoist, My Study Life, TeamSnap, or other apps tailored explicitly for athletes can help you visualize your time allocations, set reminders for classes, practices, games, and study sessions, and even share your schedule with coaches and family to ensure everyone is aligned. These tools do much more than keep you organized; they provide a platform for efficiently managing your time, allowing you to focus more on excelling both on the field and in the classroom.

For instance, consider using My Study Life or another calendar app that integrates both academic deadlines and athletic schedules. Such integration helps you see potential time conflicts and allows you to plan your workload around important matches or tournaments, ensuring you never find yourself cramming for a test the night after a taxing game. Harnessing these tools effectively starts with familiarizing yourself with their features and integrating them into your daily routine so that checking and updating your digital planner becomes as habitual as checking your sports gear before a game.

SCHEDULING PRACTICES

Creating a balanced schedule is more art than science, demanding a nuanced understanding of your physical, academic, and social needs. Start by mapping out fixed commitments like classes and training sessions. Then, allocate specific times for homework and studying. Remember, consistency is key. Try to dedicate the same time each day or week to studying to develop a routine that supports habit formation.

Next, ensure you schedule time for rest and social activities—these are not just optional extras but essential components of your overall well-being. Balancing these elements might seem daunting, but by visualizing your week in a planner, you can identify and make use of interstitial times—those small windows between commitments—for short rest periods or quick social check-ins. This way, you ensure a well-rounded routine that nurtures your academic and athletic growth while also caring for your mental and emotional health.

TIME AUDITS

Performing regular time audits is like doing a sports video analysis; it helps you identify areas where you can improve. For a week, track how you spend your time, from the major blocks of studying and training to the often-overlooked moments like scrolling through social media or chatting with friends. Reviewing this data can be eye-opening, providing insights into how much time you might be wasting on unproductive activities or how little time you allow for essential rest.

Use this analysis to adjust your schedule. You may find that you can swap half an hour of social media time for an extra study session or more sleep. Maybe you'll discover the need to be more disciplined about ending conversations with teammates after practice so you can start your homework earlier. These adjustments can significantly increase your productivity and reduce stress, as you'll feel more in control of your time and responsibilities.

BALANCING DUAL CAREERS

As a student-athlete, you are essentially managing dual careers. Recognizing this is crucial in how you approach your time management. Your sports and academic pursuits require excellence to succeed and achieve your full potential. Neither should be consistently sacrificed for the other. Communicate openly with your coaches and teachers about your dual commitments; most are willing to offer flexibility or advice if they see you are organized and proactive in managing your responsibilities.

Consider the off-season or less intense academic periods as opportunities to focus more on the other side of your dual career. For instance, you might take on more challenging coursework during the off-season when your training schedule is lighter. Conversely, reducing your academic load during the peak sports season can provide you with the bandwidth needed to excel in competitions without compromising your academic performance.

Managing these dual careers requires constant adjustment, reflection, and proactive planning. It's about making informed choices, sometimes daily, based on your priorities and performance requirements in both fields. Remember, the goal is not just to survive both worlds but to thrive, leveraging the discipline and time management skills learned in one area to benefit the other, ultimately leading to a fulfilling and successful dual career as a student-athlete.

TECHNIQUES FOR PRIORITIZING RESPONSIBILITIES

In the bustling life of a student-athlete, where every minute counts and every decision can tip the scales between stress and success, mastering the art of prioritization is crucial. You, the young athlete, are often faced with a barrage of daily tasks, from training sessions and competitions to academic deadlines and personal commitments. The key to managing this effectively lies not just in working harder but also in working smarter. This involves adopting strategic prioritization techniques that help you focus on what truly matters, ensuring that your efforts are not just busy but productive.

PRIORITIZATION METHODS

Let's start with some foundational methods that can revolutionize the way you organize your tasks. The Eisenhower Box, also known as the urgent-important matrix, is a simple yet powerful tool to help you categorize tasks based on their urgency and importance. Imagine a square divided into four smaller squares: tasks that are urgent and important go in the first box, tasks that are important but not urgent in the second, urgent but not important in the third, and neither urgent nor important in the fourth. This visual method helps you quickly see which tasks need your immediate attention, which should be planned for later, which can be delegated, and which you might be better off dropping.

EISENHOWER BOX

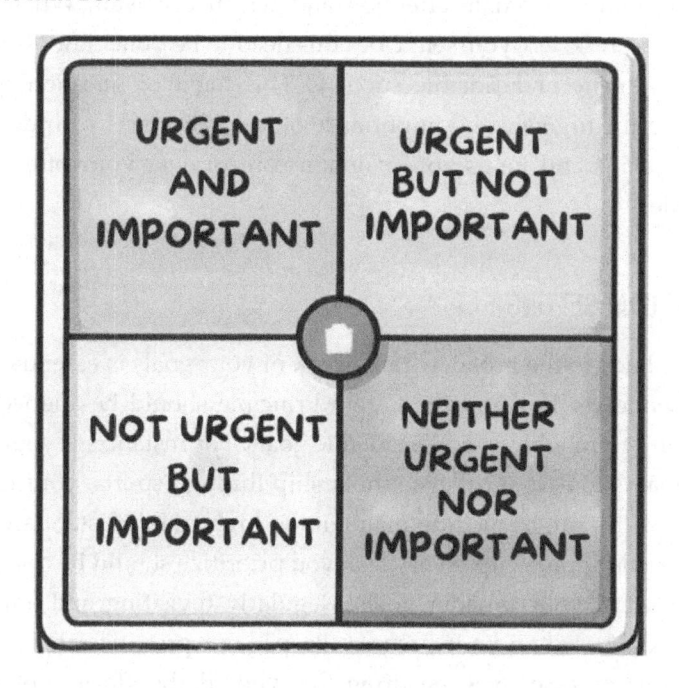

URGENT AND IMPORTANT	URGENT BUT NOT IMPORTANT
NOT URGENT BUT IMPORTANT	NEITHER URGENT NOR IMPORTANT

Another method is the Pareto Principle, or the 80/20 rule, which posits that 80% of results often come from just 20% of efforts. Applied to your life, it means identifying the 20% of your tasks or activities that contribute the most to your athletic and academic success. Once identified, focus your energy and resources on these high-impact activities, ensuring that you achieve the most significant results with the least wasted effort. This might mean prioritizing a crucial training session over an extra hour of leisure time or choosing to focus on an upcoming major exam over less critical assignments.

DECISION-MAKING SKILLS

Equipped with these prioritization frameworks, you can enhance your decision-making skills. Every day, you make numerous decisions: some trivial, some critical. By applying the urgent-important matrix, you can make informed decisions quickly, understanding which tasks deserve your immediate attention and which can wait. When faced with a new task, ask yourself: Does this need to be done now? Is it vital for my athletic or academic success? This habit of questioning and assessing the urgency and importance of tasks sharpens your decision-making skills and helps you maintain control over your often hectic schedule.

ROLE OF GOAL SETTING

Linking back to the broader framework of your goals is essential. Both the Eisenhower Box and the Pareto Principle should be aligned with your long-term athletic and academic goals. For instance, if your long-term goal is to earn a college scholarship through sports, your day-to-day priorities might include maintaining high training standards and keeping your grades up. Every task you prioritize should be a stepping stone toward your broader goals. Regularly revisiting and adjusting these goals based on your progress keeps your priorities aligned with your ultimate objectives, ensuring that your daily efforts propel you forward in the right direction.

PRACTICAL EXERCISES

To put these concepts into practice, consider engaging in scenario-based decision-making activities. These exercises simulate real-life choices you might face, such as deciding between an extra training session or preparing for an important presentation. In each scenario, apply the Eisenhower Box to categorize tasks and use the Pareto Principle to identify which actions will yield the most significant benefit toward achieving your goals. Reflect on these decisions and consider their long-term impacts on your sports and academic careers. Such practical exercises not only reinforce the theoretical knowledge of prioritization techniques but also enhance your ability to apply them under real-world pressures, ensuring you are prepared to make smart, strategic decisions in your daily life as a student-athlete.

THE ROLE OF REST AND RECOVERY IN MENTAL HEALTH

Understanding the critical role of rest and recovery in your regimen as a young athlete is foundational to both your short-term performance and long-term health. While the grind of daily training and competition is often glorified, the science behind rest illuminates its equally vital role in enhancing performance, preventing injuries, and supporting mental health. Every high-intensity workout or competition strains your muscles and your nervous system; without adequate rest, these stresses accumulate, leading to fatigue, decreased performance, and increased risk of injury. More importantly, the mental strain of continuous, intense focus without sufficient downtime can lead to burnout, a state of emotional, physical, and mental exhaustion caused by excessive and prolonged stress.

Rest is multifaceted and involves more than just getting enough sleep. It includes active recovery, passive recovery, and mental relaxation practices, each tailored to meet the unique demands placed on athletes like you. Active recovery might involve low-intensity activities such as yoga, swimming, or even a gentle jog, which help increase blood flow to your muscles, delivering nutrients needed for repair while also flushing out waste products from intense exercise. This type of recovery is particularly useful after heavy competition days, helping to reduce muscle soreness and speed up the recovery process.

Passive recovery, on the other hand, involves complete rest where no physical activity is undertaken. This can be challenging for athletes who are accustomed to constant activity, but it is essential for allowing your muscles and your nervous system to fully recover. During passive recovery, processes that are not as effective during active periods, such as protein synthesis and tissue repair, are optimized. This is also a time when the majority of muscle growth occurs, underscoring the importance of integrating complete rest days into your training schedule.

Mental relaxation practices include techniques such as meditation, guided imagery, or simply engaging in hobbies that allow you to mentally decompress. These practices aid in mental recovery and are essential for maintaining a balanced psychological state. They help manage stress, improve concentration, and reduce symptoms of anxiety and depression, contributing to overall mental wellness. Integrating mental relaxation into your daily routine can be as simple as setting aside time each day to perform deep-breathing exercises or dedicating a few evenings a week to a hobby unrelated to your sport.

SLEEP HYGIENE

Sleep is perhaps the most critical component of your recovery process. It's during sleep that your body undergoes most of its repair and recovery processes. Developing good sleep hygiene is, therefore, essential for optimizing these benefits. As a student-athlete, you should aim for 8-10 hours of quality sleep per night. This can be facilitated by establishing a consistent bedtime routine that signals to your body that it's time to wind down. Avoid stimulants like caffeine and electronics at least an hour before bed, as these can interfere with your ability to fall asleep.

Creating an environment conducive to good sleep is also crucial. Your sleep environment should be cool, quiet, and dark—conditions that support the release of melatonin, the hormone responsible for regulating sleep. Investing in a good quality mattress and pillows can also enhance sleep quality, ensuring that your body is adequately supported and can relax fully during the night.

MANAGING OVERTRAINING

Recognizing the signs of overtraining is crucial for implementing effective rest and recovery strategies. Symptoms of overtraining include persistent fatigue, decreased performance, insomnia, increased susceptibility to infections, irritability, and a general feeling of staleness. If you notice these signs, it may be an indication that you need to adjust your training load or increase your recovery time.

To manage overtraining, it's important to listen to your body and communicate openly with your coaches about how you're feeling. They can help adjust your training program to include more rest days or lighter training periods, ensuring that your body gets the recovery it needs. Additionally, incorporating regular assessments of your physical and mental state can help identify potential issues before they become serious, allowing for timely adjustments to your training and recovery plans.

Rest and recovery are not just supplementary aspects of your training; they are integral to your success as an athlete. Understanding and implementing effective rest techniques, prioritizing sleep hygiene, and managing your training load to prevent overtraining can enhance your performance, extend your athletic career, and improve your overall well-being. So, as you continue to push your limits and strive for excellence, remember that sometimes, stepping back and allowing yourself to recover is the most productive step forward.

MANAGING RELATIONSHIPS ALONGSIDE ATHLETIC COMMITMENTS

Navigating the intricate world of relationships while juggling the demands of both athletics and academics is like performing a high-wire act without a safety net. The stakes are high, and the balance is delicate. Effective communication stands as the cornerstone of maintaining healthy relationships, whether with family, friends, or teammates. As a young athlete, mastering this skill is crucial, not just for personal contentment but also for fostering a supportive environment that propels you towards your goals.

In this context, communication extends beyond just talking; it involves active listening, understanding, and responding appropriately. It's about clearly expressing your needs and schedules to those around you and equally understanding their expectations and limitations. For instance, explaining the extent of your commitments to your family can help set realistic expectations about your availability for family events. Similarly, keeping your teammates and coaches in the loop about your academic deadlines ensures they understand your occasional unavailability for extra training sessions. This open line of dialog helps prevent misunderstandings and builds a foundation of mutual respect and support.

Moreover, effective communication is pivotal when emotions run high. Sports environments can be intense, and academic pressures do not offer much respite either. Learning to convey your feelings constructively can help mitigate conflicts and strengthen relationships. Techniques such as 'I' statements (e.g., "I feel overwhelmed when practice runs late into study time") rather than accusations (e.g., "You keep us too late at practice") foster a more receptive atmosphere for addressing concerns.

Balancing your social life with your commitments to sports and studies demands more than just good communication. It requires strategic planning and the wisdom to prioritize. It's about making intentional choices about how you spend your free time, ensuring you maintain social connections without compromising your responsibilities. For example, you might choose to meet friends for a study session rather than a late-night movie, combining socializing with academic productivity. Or perhaps you decide to spend quality time with family on your rest days, which helps rejuvenate your spirit while keeping family bonds strong.

Emotional intelligence plays a crucial role in managing the dynamics of these relationships under the constant pressure of your schedule. This ability to recognize, understand, and manage not only your emotions but also those of others around you can significantly enhance how you interact with peers and family. It allows you to pick up on abnormal cues during interactions, perhaps understanding why a teammate might be upset or a friend might feel neglected. Developing your emotional intelligence can be as simple as practicing empathy, paying attention to how others respond during conversations, and adjusting your behavior to acknowledge their feelings.

A robust support network is invaluable, and cultivating it requires both effort and tact. This network should comprise individuals who understand and respect the demands placed on you as a student-athlete. They are the people who encourage you when you're down, celebrate your successes, and offer help when you're overwhelmed. Building such a network means being there for others, too; it's a reciprocal relationship where support flows both ways. Engage regularly with your support network, appreciate their efforts, and be ready to assist them in their times of need, which strengthens the bonds and ensures a mutual support system that endures.

Navigating relationships as a student-athlete is about finding harmony in the chaos of competing demands. It's about communicating effectively, making wise choices about your social engagements, understanding and managing emotions skillfully, and nurturing a supportive network. These elements are not just foundational to your success as an athlete and a student but are crucial skills that will serve you well beyond the field and the classroom. As you continue to develop these skills, remember that each interaction is an opportunity to strengthen the bonds that support and sustain you throughout your athletic and academic journey.

WHEN TO SAY NO: SETTING HEALTHY BOUNDARIES

Understanding when and how to set boundaries is crucial for maintaining your mental health and ensuring long-term success in both your athletic and personal life. As a young athlete, you are often pulled in multiple directions—whether it's training sessions, academic obligations, or social activities. Knowing when to say "no" is not just about safeguarding your time; it's about respecting your personal limits and ensuring you can give your best where it truly counts.

The importance of setting boundaries lies in the realistic acknowledgment that your energy and time are finite. Just as you can't physically train non-stop without rest, you can't commit to every demand or opportunity that comes your way without risking burnout. Effective boundary-setting helps manage the physical and emotional overload that can come from trying to do too much. It allows you to prioritize your tasks in alignment with your most significant goals—be it excelling in a crucial tournament or achieving a high academic standard.

Developing skills to set and communicate your boundaries clearly is vital. Start by identifying your priorities and limits. What are the non-negotiable aspects of your daily routine? How much time and energy can you devote to activities outside of these priorities? Once you have a clear understanding, communicate these boundaries clearly and assertively to friends, family, coaches, and even yourself. Use straightforward language, and be direct about what you can and cannot commit to. For example, if asked to participate in an additional social event during a week where you have important games and tests, you might say, "I appreciate the invite, but I need to keep my focus on my upcoming game and exam. Let's find another time to hang out."

Handling feelings of guilt and external pressures is perhaps one of the more challenging aspects of saying no. It's natural to worry about disappointing others or to fear missing out on opportunities. However, remember that saying no is often necessary to meet your higher commitments fully. To manage these feelings, remind yourself of the reasons behind your boundaries. Reaffirm your choices by considering the consequences of overcommitting—such as underperformance or increased stress. Practicing self-compassion is crucial; understand that you are making these choices not out of selfishness but out of a need to manage your responsibilities effectively.

Consider the experiences of notable athletes who have mastered the art of setting boundaries. For example, a well-known collegiate runner decided to limit her social activities significantly during the competitive season. She communicated her decision clearly to her friends, explaining that maintaining her performance level required more rest and fewer late nights. While initially challenging, this boundary allowed her to train effectively and maintain high energy levels for races. Her performance improved, and she eventually qualified for national competitions, a testament to the effectiveness of her strategy. This case underscores that while setting boundaries might require tough choices, the long-term benefits in terms of performance and personal well-being are invaluable.

. . .

As you navigate the complex demands of being a student-athlete, remember that setting healthy boundaries is a skill that will not only improve your athletic performance but also enhance your overall quality of life. It teaches you to make thoughtful decisions about how you spend your time and energy, ensuring that you are always performing at your best, both on and off the field.

CHAPTER 7
ADVANCED MENTAL TRAINING TECHNIQUES

"You miss 100% of the shots you don't take."
— Wayne Gretzky

IMAGINE STEPPING into a game where not only your physical skills are tested, but so too is your ability to maintain composure under stress. What if you could train your mind to read and respond to your body's signals like a star quarterback reading the defense and making the perfect play call? This is where advanced mental training techniques, particularly the use of biofeedback, come into play. Beyond physical training and tactical strategies, understanding and regulating your physiological responses can elevate your performance in ways you might not have considered possible.

USING BIOFEEDBACK FOR IMPROVED SELF-REGULATION

Introduction to Biofeedback

Biofeedback is a cutting-edge technique where you use electronic monitoring devices to obtain information about your body's functions, primarily to train yourself to control them consciously. By using sensors that measure your body's physiological state, biofeedback provides real-time feedback on metrics such as heart rate, muscle tension, temperature, and brainwave patterns. This feedback helps you recognize the physical manifestations of stress and anxiety, like an increased heart rate or rapid breathing, which are often subtle and overlooked until they significantly impact performance.

The relevance of this technique in sports cannot be overstated. Biofeedback empowers you, the athlete, to master the art of self-regulation—a key aspect of mental toughness. This mastery is not just about controlling nervousness before a big game; it's about optimizing your entire physiological landscape to enhance performance consistently.

TYPES OF BIOFEEDBACK

There are several types of biofeedback, each suited to different needs and objectives. Heart Rate Variability (HRV) biofeedback, for instance, measures the time interval between heartbeats, which is linked to your body's stress and relaxation responses. By training to improve your HRV, you can enhance your ability to remain calm and composed under pressure, a vital skill in high-stakes competitions.

Another significant type is Electroencephalography (EEG) biofeedback, also known as neurofeedback. This method focuses on your brain's electrical activity, helping you understand and regulate your brain waves to improve concentration, reduce anxiety, and enhance cognitive functions. For athletes, this can mean better focus during a game, quicker decision-making, and improved motor coordination.

TRAINING SELF-REGULATION

Learning to use biofeedback effectively involves training sessions with a qualified practitioner who guides you through exercises aimed at controlling specific physiological functions. For example, you might use HRV biofeedback to learn how to slow your heart rate through controlled breathing or use EEG biofeedback to practice entering a state of calm focus before a performance.

The process is similar to physical training, requiring regular practice and consistency. Just as you would lift weights to build muscle, you train with biofeedback to strengthen your mind's ability to control your body's responses to stress. Over time, these sessions help you develop a heightened awareness of your physiological state and the ability to adjust it consciously, enhancing both your mental and physical performance in sports.

CASE STUDIES AND EXAMPLES

Consider the case of a collegiate swimmer who struggled with pre-race anxiety. Despite being physically well-prepared, her performance was inconsistent, often hindered by nerves at crucial moments. Through HRV biofeedback training, she learned to manage her anxiety by controlling her breathing and heart rate. This training improved her race starts and overall performance, leading to personal bests and more consistent finishes.

Another example is a professional golfer who used EEG biofeedback to improve his concentration during long tournaments. By learning to regulate his brain waves, he enhanced his ability to stay focused throughout each round, reducing mental fatigue and improving his shot precision under pressure.

Similarly, think of a baseball pitcher who struggled with maintaining composure during high-pressure situations. Despite having excellent technique and physical conditioning, his performance would falter during crucial innings. Through mindfulness and HRV biofeedback training, he learned to control his stress response, maintain a steady heart rate, and focus his mind. This resulted in improved pitch accuracy and consistency, especially during the most demanding parts of the game.

These examples underscore the practical benefits of biofeedback in sports, demonstrating how athletes can significantly enhance their performance by incorporating advanced mental training techniques into their routines. By understanding and regulating the mind-body connection, athletes open up new possibilities for peak performance, transforming potential barriers into opportunities for growth and success.

ADVANCED VISUALIZATION TECHNIQUES FOR ELITE PERFORMANCE

Visualization, a technique familiar to many athletes, involves mentally rehearsing specific actions or outcomes to enhance performance. While basic visualization might involve seeing yourself crossing the finish line or making a successful shot, advanced visualization techniques dive much deeper. These methods refine your mental imagery and integrate a richer sensory experience, making your mental rehearsals as detailed and realistic as possible. This depth of practice is crucial for high-performance athletes like you, who need every edge they can get to excel in competitive environments.

Expanding on basic visualization, let's explore more intricate imagery practices tailored specifically for athletes aiming to reach elite levels. One effective method is to incorporate dynamic and complex scenarios into your visualization. For instance, instead of merely imagining the act of scoring a goal, visualize the entire play leading up to that moment. See in your mind's eye the positioning of other players, hear the crowd's roar, feel the grip of your footwear on the turf, and even smell the fresh grass or the sweat of competition. This type of detailed visualization helps prepare you for real-game situations, enhancing your decision-making skills and reaction times because you've mentally rehearsed various scenarios and their potential outcomes.

SENSORY INTEGRATION IN VISUALIZATION

To deepen the impact of your visualization practices, engaging all your senses is essential. When you visualize an event, try to construct the scenario with as much sensory detail as possible. For example, if you're a sprinter, feel the explosive start from the blocks, hear the sound of your breath and footsteps, see the finish line approaching, and even taste the tang of adrenaline in your mouth. This multisensory approach makes the visualization more engaging and more closely mirrors real-life experiences, which can enhance your neural connections related to the sport, leading to improvements in physical performance.

Practicing these techniques regularly can indirectly influence your muscle memory. The brain doesn't distinguish well between vividly imagined and actual experiences; thus, by repeatedly visualizing complex, sensory-rich scenarios, you're priming your body to react as it has rehearsed mentally. This preparation can be particularly advantageous during high-pressure situations where automatic, finely-tuned responses are crucial.

SCENARIO-BASED VISUALIZATION

Another advanced technique is scenario-based visualization, which involves imagining various possible scenarios you might encounter during competition, including best-case and worst-case situations. This form of visualization prepares you for the unpredictability of sports. For instance, imagine you're in a tennis match facing a particularly tough opponent. Visualize triumphing in straight sets, coming back from a set down, dealing with bad line calls, or managing crowd distractions. By mentally rehearsing how you'd handle these situations, you develop a toolkit of psychological responses that you can draw upon when facing similar real challenges.

This technique enhances your adaptability and resilience, qualities that define elite athletes. It trains you to maintain focus and composure regardless of the circumstances, ensuring that you are never caught off guard and always prepared to perform at your best.

REGULAR PRACTICE AND APPLICATION

The key to reaping the full benefits of advanced visualization techniques is consistent practice. Integrate these practices into your daily training routine and pre-competition preparations. Dedicate specific times for mental rehearsals, treating them with the same seriousness as physical training sessions. Regularly engaging in detailed, sensory-rich visualizations enhances their effectiveness, making the imagined scenarios increasingly vivid and the derived benefits more impactful.

To effectively incorporate these visualization practices, start each session with a clear objective. Decide which skills or scenarios you want to focus on and use guided imagery to create detailed mental simulations. Post-visualization, reflect on the experience. Consider what felt real and what didn't, and how you can enhance the realism next time. This reflective practice not only improves your visualization skills but also deepens your understanding of your mental and emotional landscape during competition, providing insights that are invaluable for personal growth and performance enhancement.

By advancing your visualization skills through detailed, sensory-integrated, and scenario-based techniques and by making this practice a regular part of your training, you equip yourself with a powerful tool that prepares you mentally for competition. This preparation is crucial, as mental readiness often differentiates good athletes from great ones. So, as you continue to train and compete, remember that your mind is as potent a tool as your body in achieving athletic excellence. Through diligent practice of these advanced visualization techniques, you are setting the stage for peak performances that are as mentally fabricated as they are physically executed.

COGNITIVE BEHAVIORAL APPROACHES TO ENHANCE MENTAL TOUGHNESS

Cognitive Behavioral Therapy (CBT) is a form of psychological treatment that has proven effective in a range of issues, including anxiety, depression, and even performance anxiety in sports. Its principles are based on the interconnectedness of thoughts, emotions, and behaviors, suggesting that altering one can substantially impact others. For athletes, CBT offers tools to manage negative thoughts and behaviors that might impede performance, turning psychological barriers into springboards for success.

CBT in sports psychology focuses primarily on helping athletes develop mental strategies that promote healthy thought patterns, enhancing both mental resilience and performance. Imagine you're preparing for a crucial match, and a thought crosses your mind: "I'm not good enough to win." Such a thought can trigger a cascade of negative emotions and potentially harmful behaviors like withdrawing effort or giving up. CBT tackles these negative thoughts by challenging their validity and systematically reshaping them into more constructive ones.

Identifying and challenging cognitive distortions—a common CBT technique—requires you to first become aware of the specific types of distorted thinking you engage in. Common distortions in athletics include "all-or-nothing" thinking (e.g., viewing a performance as entirely good or bad with no middle ground) and "catastrophizing" (e.g., blowing a small mistake out of proportion). By learning to identify when you're slipping into these patterns, you can begin to counter them. For instance, if you tend to think in "all-or-nothing" terms, a strategy might be to evaluate your performance based on a range of criteria rather than a single outcome. This helps create a more balanced view of your abilities and efforts, reducing unnecessary pressure and enhancing your focus.

Furthermore, CBT encourages the use of behavioral experiments, which are structured activities designed to test the beliefs you hold about your abilities and the outcomes of your actions. These experiments can be particularly enlightening, as they often reveal that the outcomes you fear are either not as likely or as catastrophic as you imagine. For example, you might avoid taking risks during a game because you believe it will lead to mistakes and criticism. A behavioral experiment might involve intentionally taking calculated risks during practice to observe the actual consequences. More often than not, you'll find that the outcome is less severe than expected and sometimes even positive, leading to increased confidence and a willingness to engage more fully in competitive situations.

Integrating CBT techniques into your regular training routine can be done through mental skills training sessions that focus on cognitive exercises before or after physical practice. Regular sessions can help solidify these skills, making them second nature. Coaches can facilitate this integration by incorporating brief CBT-based discussions into practice sessions, focusing on identifying unhelpful thoughts athletes might have had during the day and using CBT techniques to address them. This not only enhances individual mental toughness but can also uplift the overall psychological resilience of the team.

By incorporating CBT into your mental training, you equip yourself with a powerful set of tools to control and use your thoughts to your advantage. Rather than being buffeted by negative thoughts and emotions, you learn to navigate them strategically, enhancing your performance and enjoyment in your sport. This approach does not just apply to your time on the track, field, or court; it's a skill set that benefits all areas of life, providing a robust framework for tackling challenges and achieving personal goals.

INTEGRATING TECHNOLOGY IN MENTAL TRAINING

In your quest to sharpen your mental game and boost your performance, embracing the latest technologies like virtual reality (VR), augmented reality (AR), and various mobile apps can dramatically transform how you train mentally. These technologies are not just gadgets with cool features; they are essential tools that can simulate training environments, provide critical feedback in real time, and help you practice mental strategies effectively.

Virtual reality, particularly, has revolutionized mental training for athletes. By creating a completely immersive environment, VR allows you to practice under game-like conditions without the physical wear and tear or the logistical constraints of traditional training. For example, imagine you're a downhill skier, and you have the ability to run the course hundreds of times in a virtual setting before you ever set foot on the actual slope. This repeated exposure not only builds familiarity and confidence but also allows you to experiment with different techniques and strategies that you can later apply in real competitions.

Augmented reality also plays a crucial role by overlaying digital information in the real training environment. Unlike VR, AR enhances the world around you without creating an entirely artificial environment. For instance, AR can be used in football training to overlay the trajectory of a football on a quarterback's visor, helping them make better throws in practice that translate to improved performance during games. These AR applications enhance real-world training by providing additional information that would not otherwise be available.

Mobile apps that specialize in mental skills training are another resource at your disposal. These apps can guide you through various mental training exercises, track your progress, and even connect you with mental coaches. They provide convenience and accessibility, allowing you to engage in mental training exercises anytime and anywhere, which is perfect for your busy schedule. Some apps also use gamification to make mental training more engaging, offering rewards and incentives that encourage regular practice.

The benefits of incorporating these technologies into your training regimen are manifold. Firstly, they increase engagement. Training with technology is often more interactive and enjoyable, which can keep you motivated and committed to your mental training program. Personalized feedback provided by these technologies can also be a game-changer. For instance, VR and AR systems can track your eye movement, body language, and other physiological indicators to provide feedback that's specifically tailored to your needs, helping you make precise adjustments to your mental approach.

CASE STUDIES OF TECHNOLOGY USE

Consider the example of a collegiate basketball team that integrated VR into their training protocol. The coaches used VR to simulate high-pressure game scenarios for their players, including free-throw shooting with a simulated full crowd and noise. Over the season, players who trained with VR demonstrated significant improvements in their free-throw accuracy and reported feeling more confident during actual games. The immersive nature of VR helped them adjust to the intense pressure of real competitions, enhancing their overall performance.

Another case involves a professional golfer who used AR glasses to improve her putting skills. The AR system projected the ideal putting line on her glasses based on the contour of the green, helping her visualize the perfect putt during practice. This visualization technique, practiced repeatedly, translated into more consistent performance during tournaments, particularly under challenging conditions.

These examples underscore the practical benefits and versatility of these technologies in enhancing athletic performance through superior mental training.

GUIDELINES FOR EFFECTIVE USE

To effectively integrate these technologies into your mental training program, start by identifying your specific needs and the areas of your mental game that need the most improvement. This tailored approach ensures that the technology you choose aligns with your personal training goals. It's also crucial to balance technology use with traditional training methods. While tech-based training can provide unique advantages, it should complement rather than replace traditional mental training techniques.

Remember, it's important to avoid becoming overwhelmed by the high-tech aspects of these tools. Begin slowly, incorporating one technology at a time and getting comfortable with it before introducing another. This step-by-step approach helps you integrate each new tool effectively without feeling overwhelmed.

Incorporating technology into your training routine represents a proactive approach to mental training that leverages cutting-edge tools to enhance your performance. By utilizing VR, AR, and mobile apps, you not only stay ahead of the curve in athletic training but also set a foundation for continual improvement and success in your sport. As you move forward, keep exploring new technologies and adapting them to your training needs, ensuring that your mental game is as sharp and effective as your physical performance.

PERIODIZATION OF MENTAL TRAINING: PLANNING FOR PEAK PERFORMANCE

Periodization in mental training is a strategic approach to developing mental skills that are critical for peak performance in sports. Much like physical training, mental skills should be developed appropriately, and follow a structured and phased approach that aligns with your overall training and competition cycle. The essence of periodization is to systematically plan your mental training to ensure that you are mentally prepared to perform your best when it matters most.

The concept of periodization involves dividing the training calendar into specific phases, each with particular goals and focuses. For mental training, this means adapting your psychological strategies and exercises according to the phase of training you are in. For example, during the off-season, the focus might be on developing foundational mental skills such as concentration and stress management. As you move into the pre-season and in-season phases, the emphasis shifts towards more specific skills like mental rehearsal and game-day preparation strategies.

Creating a periodized mental training program starts with understanding your athletic calendar and identifying key competitions and training phases. This understanding allows you to tailor your mental training to meet the demands of each phase. For instance, during the off-season, you might work on building resilience and mental toughness through exercises that challenge your comfort zones. This could involve training under different environmental conditions or practicing mindfulness to enhance focus.

As you transition into the pre-season, the mental training shifts towards more specific preparations for competition. This phase might focus on setting performance goals, enhancing motivation, and fine-tuning your mental routines. Visualization techniques become crucial here as you begin to mentally rehearse specific competition scenarios and strategies. This phase prepares you mentally to handle the pressures and expectations of upcoming competitions.

PHASES OF MENTAL TRAINING

Once the regular season begins, maintaining and optimizing mental performance becomes the priority. In-season mental training is about applying and adjusting the strategies you've developed in the off-season and pre-season. It's also about mental maintenance—keeping your cognitive and emotional skills sharp and ready for competition. Techniques such as in-game focus strategies, emotional regulation during high-pressure moments, and post-competition analysis are key components of this phase.

Monitoring and adjusting your mental training throughout these phases is critical. Just as you would adjust your physical training based on performance outcomes, the same applies to mental training. Regularly assessing how well your mental strategies are working allows you to make necessary adjustments. For example, suppose you find that your pre-game routine isn't effectively calming your nerves. In that case, you might tweak it or try alternative relaxation techniques. Feedback from coaches, teammates, and personal reflection all play a role in this evaluative process.

Effective monitoring involves both subjective assessments, such as self-reported levels of confidence or focus, and objective measures, such as performance outcomes or physiological indicators obtained through biofeedback. By consistently evaluating the effectiveness of your mental training, you ensure that your mental preparation aligns with your physical readiness, leading to optimal performance when you compete.

Integrating periodization into your mental training enhances your ability to perform under pressure and contributes to your long-term development as an athlete. By systematically building and refining your mental skills, you ensure that your psychological resilience grows along with your physical abilities. This holistic approach to training prepares you for the rigors of competition and the challenges of maintaining peak performance over time.

. . .

As this chapter wraps up, reflect on how periodization can transform your mental training from a sporadic, sometimes overlooked aspect of your preparation to a core component of your athletic development. The structured approach to building mental toughness and readiness we've discussed here is not just about preparing for the next game or season but about cultivating a mindset geared towards continual growth and peak performance. As you move forward, carry these strategies with you, applying them systematically to reach and maintain your best mental and physical form. Next, we'll explore how integrating nutrition, rest, and recovery strategies can further enhance your performance and overall well-being, rounding out your comprehensive approach to training.

CHAPTER 8
NUTRITION, REST, AND MENTAL PERFORMANCE

"Exercise is king. Nutrition is queen. Put them together and you've got a kingdom."
— Jack LaLanne

IMAGINE STEPPING up to the starting line, your muscles primed and your focus sharp. Now, consider the fuel that powers both that physical readiness and mental clarity. It's not just the hours of training but what's on your plate that shapes your performance. This chapter delves into the critical role of nutrition in enhancing mental function, ensuring you're as sharp mentally as you are physically. We explore the vital nutrients that serve as the building blocks for your brain's optimal performance, practical advice on when and how to supplement your diet, and the strategic timing of nutrient intake to align perfectly with your training and competition schedules.

ESSENTIAL NUTRIENTS FOR OPTIMAL MENTAL FUNCTION

Understanding Micronutrients and Macronutrients

Before diving into the specifics of how nutrition impacts mental performance, it's important to understand the basics of micronutrients and macronutrients.

MICRONUTRIENTS

Micronutrients are vitamins and minerals required by the body in small amounts. Despite their relatively low required quantities, they are vital for overall health and optimal functioning of the body and brain.

VITAMINS

These organic compounds are crucial for various biochemical processes. They support immune function, energy production, and blood clotting, among other roles.

Key vitamins include:

- **Vitamin A:** Important for vision, immune function, and skin health. Sources include carrots, sweet potatoes, and spinach.
- **Vitamin B Complex:** Includes vitamins like B1 (thiamine), B2 (riboflavin), B3 (niacin), B6, B9 (folate), and B12. These are essential for energy production and the formation of red blood cells. Sources include whole grains, meats, and dairy products.
- **Vitamin C:** Necessary for the repair of tissues and enzymatic production of certain neurotransmitters. Sources include citrus fruits, strawberries, and bell peppers.
- **Vitamin D:** Supports bone health by aiding calcium absorption. Sources include sunlight, fortified dairy products, and fatty fish.
- **Vitamin E:** Acts as an antioxidant, protecting cells from damage. Sources include nuts, seeds, and green leafy vegetables.

MINERALS

Inorganic elements that also play a crucial role in various bodily functions.

Important minerals include:

- **Calcium:** Essential for healthy bones and teeth, muscle function, and nerve signaling. Sources include dairy products, fortified plant milks, and leafy greens.
- **Iron:** Critical for the formation of hemoglobin, which carries oxygen in the blood. Sources include red meat, beans, and fortified cereals.
- **Magnesium:** Involved in over 300 biochemical reactions in the body, including muscle and nerve function. Sources include nuts, whole grains, and spinach.
- **Zinc:** Supports immune function, protein synthesis, and wound healing. Sources include meat, shellfish, and legumes.

MACRONUTRIENTS

Macronutrients are nutrients required in larger quantities and provide the energy needed for daily activities and bodily functions. They include carbohydrates, proteins, and fats.

- **Carbohydrates:** Carbohydrates are the primary energy source for both the brain and muscles. Carbohydrates are broken down into glucose, which fuels brain and muscle activity. They should constitute about 45-65% of daily calorie intake. Young athletes should consume 5-7 grams of carbohydrates per kilogram of body weight daily for moderate training and 7-10 grams per kilogram for intense

training. Good sources include whole grains, fruits, vegetables, and legumes.
- **Proteins:** Essential for building and repairing tissues, including muscles, and are crucial for the production of enzymes and hormones. Proteins also support neurotransmitter production and overall brain function. Proteins should make up about 10-35% of daily calorie intake, with young athletes aiming for 1.2 to 2.0 grams per kilogram of body weight daily. Sources include lean meats, fish, eggs, dairy products, and, to some extent, legumes and nuts.
- **Fats:** Important for brain health, energy storage, and hormone production. Healthy fats should account for about 20-35% of daily calorie intake, with young athletes focusing on 0.5-1.5 grams of fat per kilogram of body weight daily. Sources include avocados, nuts, seeds, olive oil, and fatty fish like salmon and mackerel.

IDENTIFY KEY NUTRIENTS

To maintain peak mental performance, your brain requires a diverse array of nutrients. Omega-3 fatty acids, for instance, are crucial for maintaining the structure and function of your brain cells. Found abundantly in fish like salmon and sardines, these fats are vital for cognitive function, including memory and mood regulation. Antioxidants, which combat oxidative stress that can damage brain cells, are another group of vital nutrients. They are plentiful in berries, nuts, and leafy greens, protecting your brain from the wear and tear that comes with intense training and competition.

Vitamins such as B-complex, C, and E play multiple roles in brain health. B vitamins, found in whole grains, meat, and dairy, are pivotal in energy production and the synthesis of neurotransmitters, which are chemical messengers that carry signals between nerve cells in your brain. Vitamin C, abundant in citrus fruits and vegetables like bell peppers, supports not only general health but also your brain's cognitive capacities. Vitamin E, with its powerful antioxidant properties, helps protect your brain against oxidative stress; it's readily available in nuts and seeds.

Minerals like zinc and magnesium also contribute significantly to neurological functions. Zinc, which you can get from meat, shellfish, and legumes, aids in nerve signaling and cognitive stability. Magnesium, present in nuts, whole grains, and spinach, is essential for nerve function and mood regulation. Together, these nutrients ensure that your brain has all it needs to manage the complexities and pressures of competitive sports.

SOURCES OF NUTRIENTS

Incorporating these nutrients into your diet isn't just about picking the right foods; it's about understanding how these foods can be combined to support cognitive health. For omega-3 fatty acids, seafood is an excellent source, but for vegetarians, flaxseeds and walnuts are good alternatives. Antioxidants can be easily integrated into your diet through colorful fruits and vegetables. To ensure adequate intake of B vitamins, focus on maintaining a balanced diet that includes a variety of whole grains, proteins, and dairy products. Nuts and seeds are not just snacks; they are great sources of both Vitamin E and magnesium, essential for your brain's resilience and recovery.

NUTRIENT TIMING

The timing of nutrient intake can be as critical as the nutrients themselves, especially in relation to your training and competition schedules. Consuming carbohydrates and proteins before training can provide you with the energy needed for endurance and the building blocks for muscle recovery. Post-training, your focus should shift to recovery - here, antioxidants and proteins can help repair muscle damage and reduce inflammation. Before competitions, a meal rich in complex carbohydrates and moderate in proteins can ensure a steady energy supply, while B vitamins can help maintain optimal neurological function during the stress of performance.

SUPPLEMENTATION ADVICE

While a balanced diet is the best way to meet your nutritional needs, supplementation can be beneficial in certain situations. For instance, if dietary restrictions or preferences limit your intake of crucial nutrients like omega-3s or B vitamins, supplements might be necessary. However, the key is choosing high-quality supplements and consulting with healthcare professionals to ensure they are necessary and suitable for your specific needs. This ensures that supplementation is both safe and effective, supporting your mental and physical health without compromising your dietary balance.

Understanding and implementing nutritional strategies to support mental performance is crucial for any athlete. By focusing on nutrient-rich foods, considering the timing of their intake, and supplementing wisely, you can ensure that your diet supports both your mental and physical demands, keeping you competitive and sharp in every arena.

THE SCIENCE OF SLEEP AND PERFORMANCE

Understanding how sleep works is like uncovering the secret playbook of your body's recovery and mental acuity processes. Each night, your brain cycles through several stages of sleep, each serving a unique function in supporting both your mental and physical recovery. The stages of sleep can be broadly categorized into REM (rapid eye movement) sleep and non-REM sleep, each playing a crucial role in athletic recovery and performance. Non-REM sleep kicks off your sleep cycle and is divided into three stages, with each stage progressively deepening. The third stage, often referred to as deep sleep, is particularly vital for physical recovery. It's during this stage that the body repairs muscle, consolidates immune function, and restores energy. Following these stages, REM sleep occurs, characterized by rapid eye movement, increased brain activity, and vivid dreams. This stage is crucial for mental processes, including emotional regulation, learning, and memory consolidation. For athletes like you, both deep and REM sleep are essential as they collectively refurbish the mind and body—preparing you for both mental strategizing and physical exertion.

The impact of sleep quality and quantity extends directly to your performance on the field or court. A well-rested brain functions optimally, enhancing your decision-making abilities, reaction times, and emotional control during high-pressure moments. Consider how a well-timed pass in a basketball game or a strategic decision during a race can be influenced by your alertness and mental clarity—attributes honed by adequate sleep. Conversely, sleep deprivation can lead to slower reaction times, impaired judgment, and fluctuating moods, which can undermine your performance and increase the risk of errors and injuries. Thus, prioritizing good sleep isn't just about feeling rested; it's about setting the stage for peak mental and physical performance.

For athletes striving to optimize their sleep, establishing robust sleep hygiene practices is key. This includes maintaining a consistent sleep schedule that aligns with your training and competition demands, ensuring you get 7-9 hours of quality sleep each night. Consistency not only helps regulate your body's internal clock but also enhances the quality of sleep, allowing you to cycle through all stages of sleep adequately. Optimizing your sleep environment is another crucial strategy. This means making your bedroom conducive to sleep—cool, quiet, and dark. Invest in blackout curtains, perhaps a white noise machine, and ensure your mattress and pillows support a comfortable night's sleep. In addition, developing a pre-sleep routine can significantly enhance your sleep quality. Engaging in relaxing activities such as reading, light stretching, or meditation before bed can help signal to your body that it's time to wind down, making it easier to fall asleep and stay asleep.

Handling sleep challenges is particularly relevant for athletes, who often face unique pressures and schedules that can disrupt normal sleep patterns. Pre-competition anxiety, for instance, is a common issue that can keep you awake, filled with nervous energy about the upcoming event. Developing relaxation techniques such as deep breathing exercises or using visualization to calmly walk through the event's steps can mitigate this anxiety, promoting better sleep. Travel disruptions present another challenge, especially when crossing time zones which can disrupt your internal clock. To manage this, gradually adjust your sleep schedule a few days before traveling to align closer with the destination time zone, and try to get exposure to natural light during the day to help reset your internal clock upon arrival. These strategies ensure you remain at the top of your game, both mentally and physically, ready to tackle the challenges of your sport with vigor and vitality.

By understanding and harnessing the science of sleep, you empower yourself to perform at your best, knowing that each night's rest is a building block towards achieving and sustaining peak athletic performance.

HYDRATION AND ITS EFFECTS ON COGNITIVE FUNCTION

Body Hydration and Brain Health

Imagine your brain as an athlete in itself—requiring hydration to perform at its peak during both training and competitions. The brain is approximately 75% water, and even a slight dip in hydration levels can affect its function significantly. When you're dehydrated, your brain actually shrinks in volume. This shrinkage increases the space between your brain and skull, making your brain work harder to perform at its usual capacity, which can lead to a decrease in cognitive functions such as focus, memory retention, and decision-making skills. Additionally, dehydration impacts your mood, often leading to increased feelings of anxiety and fatigue, which can further impair your mental performance and overall mood stability during both practices and key competitions.

To put this into perspective, consider how a basketball player needs precision for shooting hoops; similarly, your brain requires optimal hydration to 'shoot' neurotransmitters effectively across synapses. Dehydration slows down the neurotransmission process, leading to slower reaction times and reduced cognitive functions. This is particularly critical in sports where split-second decisions can be the difference between winning and losing. Moreover, dehydration can lead to increased cortisol levels, the stress hormone, which not only affects your brain function but also your overall health and athletic performance by contributing to quicker onset of fatigue and reduced recovery rates.

DAILY HYDRATION GUIDELINES

For young athletes like you, maintaining hydration isn't just about drinking water during practice or games. It's about consistently keeping your body hydrated throughout the day. A general rule of thumb is to drink approximately half an ounce to an ounce of water for each pound you weigh, every day. However, factors like climate, the intensity of your training, and individual sweat rates can adjust this requirement. For instance, if you are training in hot and humid conditions or if you're involved in a high-intensity sport that induces more sweat, your hydration needs will be on the higher end of this scale.

It is also important to start your training sessions or competitions in a hydrated state. This means drinking water throughout the day leading up to your sports activities. A good practice is to drink about 14-20 ounces of water about 1-2 hours before your activity to ensure your body is adequately pre-hydrated. Then, continue to sip small amounts frequently during the event to replace the fluids lost through sweat.

MONITORING HYDRATION

Keeping track of your hydration status is essential and can be done through simple methods. One of the most straightforward ways is to pay attention to the color of your urine. A pale yellow color typically indicates proper hydration, while a dark yellow or amber color suggests dehydration. This method is an effective and immediate way to assess your hydration levels anytime during the day.

Another method involves monitoring your body weight before and after significant training sessions. Weight loss immediately after a workout is likely from fluid loss, so you should aim to replenish this by drinking about 16-24 ounces of water for every pound lost. This method not only helps in maintaining optimal hydration but also aids in recovery by ensuring that your muscles are well-hydrated and less prone to cramps and spasms.

HYDRATION STRATEGIES

Developing effective hydration strategies for both training and competition days is crucial. Begin by integrating hydration into your daily routine. Carry a water bottle with you throughout the day to remind you to keep sipping. You might also consider flavoring your water with natural fruit juices or using an electrolyte supplement to enhance taste and replenish salts lost through sweat, making hydration more appealing.

On training or competition days, structure your hydration as part of your performance strategy. Start by pre-hydrating, as mentioned above, and then use breaks in the game or practice sessions to maintain hydration. Post-activity, focus on rehydration, especially if your next training session is within 12 hours. If you find regular water monotonous, coconut water or electrolyte-infused waters can be effective alternatives that provide not just hydration but also recovery benefits.

By understanding the critical role of hydration in brain function and overall performance and by implementing strategic hydration practices, you empower yourself to perform at your best, both mentally and physically. Remember, staying hydrated is key not just to survive the rigors of intense sports but to thrive in them, making every move count towards achieving your athletic goals.

BALANCING DIET AND MENTAL HEALTH FOR YOUNG ATHLETES

Understanding the intricate relationship between diet and mental health is pivotal for you as a young athlete striving for both physical prowess and mental sharpness. The foods you consume don't just fuel your physical activities; they significantly impact your mood, energy levels, and stress resilience. For instance, carbohydrates increase the production of serotonin, a neurotransmitter that boosts mood and reduces stress. However, not all carbs are created equal. Complex carbohydrates like whole grains release glucose slowly, helping maintain stable energy levels and mood.

On the other hand, simple sugars can lead to spikes and crashes in blood sugar levels, which might cause fluctuations in your mood and energy. Including protein in your meals can enhance dopamine and norepinephrine levels, which help keep you alert and improve concentration. Meanwhile, insufficient intake of essential nutrients like omega-3 fatty acids has been linked to increased risks of mood disorders.

The pressures of maintaining peak physical condition can sometimes lead to unhealthy eating behaviors, especially in sports that emphasize specific weight categories or aesthetic aspects. It's crucial to recognize the signs of potential eating disorders, which can include excessive preoccupation with weight, extreme dieting, binge eating, or purging. These behaviors not only undermine your mental and physical health but can also severely impact your athletic performance. Promoting a healthy relationship with food involves understanding these risks and fostering an environment where you can discuss and manage these pressures constructively. Coaches, parents, and teammates play a supportive role in recognizing early signs of disordered eating and encouraging timely intervention by professionals.

Incorporating mindful eating practices can significantly enhance your dietary habits and overall well-being. Mindful eating involves paying full attention to the experience of eating and drinking, both inside and outside the body. It encourages you to notice how foods smell, taste, and feel in your mouth, as well as the effects they have on feelings and sensations in your body. This practice helps develop a greater awareness of hunger and satiety cues, which can prevent overeating and under-eating. It can be particularly beneficial during high-pressure periods, such as before competitions when nervousness might affect your eating patterns. By eating mindfully, you can maintain a balanced diet, which in turn supports optimal mental function.

Planning your nutrition meticulously can further enhance both your mental and physical performance. Developing a balanced weekly meal plan that considers your training schedule, competition dates, and academic commitments can help ensure you receive the nutrients necessary for all aspects of your life. This plan should include a variety of nutrient-dense foods to support cognitive function and muscle recovery. For instance, breakfasts rich in protein and healthy fats can provide sustained energy for morning training, while dinners rich in carbohydrates can replenish glycogen stores after intense workouts. Additionally, incorporating snacks that blend proteins, fats, and carbohydrates can provide quick energy and aid recovery between workouts and classes. Tailoring this plan to your personal preferences and dietary needs, possibly with the help of a nutritionist, ensures that you not only meet your nutritional goals but also enjoy what you eat, which is crucial for long-term adherence to any dietary plan.

By understanding and implementing these strategies, you can ensure your diet supports not only your physical demands as an athlete but also enhances your mental well-being. This holistic approach to nutrition helps safeguard your health, optimizes your performance, and ensures you can tackle the challenges of competitive sports with vigor and resilience.

PRE-COMPETITION MEALS FOR MAXIMUM MENTAL SHARPNESS

Timing your meals before a competition is crucial, not just to fuel your body but to ensure your mind is as sharp as possible. Ideally, your last major meal should be consumed approximately 3 to 4 hours before your event. This timing allows your body to digest the food sufficiently, ensuring that the energy from the meal is available during your competition while also preventing any gastrointestinal discomfort that could distract you or hinder your performance. Additionally, a small, carbohydrate-rich snack 30 to 60 minutes before the event can help top off your energy stores, especially if your competition is lengthy or particularly intense.

The composition of your pre-competition meal is vital for maintaining energy levels and cognitive function throughout your event. An effective meal should include a balance of carbohydrates, proteins, and fats. Carbohydrates are your body's primary energy source. They should make up about 60-70% of your meal to ensure you have ample glycogen stores for both endurance and high-intensity spurts. Sources like whole-grain pasta, brown rice, or quinoa provide sustained energy release. Protein is crucial for muscle repair and recovery, making up about 15-20% of the meal. Good protein sources include lean meats like chicken or fish, or for vegetarian athletes, options such as lentils or chickpeas. Fats should be consumed in moderation, comprising about 15-20% of the meal, with a focus on healthy fats like those found in avocados or nuts, which can aid in sustained energy release and satiety.

Let's consider practical examples of pre-competition meals tailored for different scenarios. For morning competitions, a breakfast of oatmeal topped with berries and a side of scrambled eggs provides a balanced mix of complex carbs, protein, and antioxidants, perfect for long-lasting energy and mental clarity. If your event is in the afternoon, a lunch of grilled chicken breast with a quinoa salad mixed with vegetables, dressed lightly with olive oil, offers an excellent balance of macros, ensuring you're fueled and ready. For evening events, a dinner of whole-grain pasta with a lean protein source like turkey meatballs and a side of steamed broccoli works well to keep you feeling full and focused.

Adapting your meal strategy based on personal experience and performance feedback is key. Each athlete's body reacts differently to foods, and what works for one might not work for another. Pay close attention to how you feel during your training and competitions relative to what you've eaten beforehand. Adjust portions, timing, and ingredients based on your observations and how your body responds. For instance, if you find yourself feeling sluggish after consuming a heavy meal of pasta and meat sauce, try reducing the portion of pasta or substituting some of the pasta with a lighter vegetable like spiralized zucchini. Continuously refining your pre-competition meal strategy in this way will help you find the ideal formula that maximizes your mental sharpness and physical performance.

Nutrition is not just fuel; it's a crucial tool for ensuring your body and mind are in peak condition for competition. By carefully selecting, timing, and balancing your meals, you can enhance your mental clarity and focus, giving you an edge over your competitors. As we wrap up this chapter on the role of nutrition, rest, and hydration in mental performance, remember that each element is interconnected. Your diet supports your physical training and recovery, hydration keeps both your mind and body sharp, and adequate rest ensures you can perform at your best. Moving forward, we'll explore strategies for managing stress and emotions, further enhancing your ability to maintain focus and perform under pressure.

CHAPTER 9
PARENT AND COACH SUPPORT STRATEGIES

"The way a team plays as a whole determines its success. You may have the greatest bunch of individual stars in the world, but if they don't play together, the club won't be worth a dime."
– Babe Ruth

IMAGINE you're a coach standing on the sidelines or a parent in the stands, watching as a young athlete pushes through the barriers of exhaustion, doubt, and pressure. What can you do to ensure these young competitors not only survive but thrive under the intense spotlight of competition? This chapter delates into the pivotal roles coaches, and parents play in nurturing mental toughness and resilience in young athletes, offering practical strategies and insights that transform the typical coaching paradigm into one that fosters mental strength and team cohesion.

COACHING TECHNIQUES THAT FOSTER MENTAL TOUGHNESS

Incorporate Mental Skills Training

For coaches, the traditional focus on physical skills and strategies is an undeniable part of athletic training; however, integrating mental skills training into your regular practice sessions can be a game-changer. Techniques such as visualization, goal-setting, and positive self-talk are not just supplementary; they are core components of a well-rounded athlete's regimen. Imagine guiding your team through a visualization session where they see themselves executing perfect plays or overcoming previous mistakes with grace and strategy. Such mental rehearsals not only enhance physical performance but also bolster psychological readiness, which is crucial in high-pressure game situations.

Encouraging athletes to set personal and team goals can also profoundly impact their mental toughness. These goals should be specific, measurable, achievable, relevant, and time-bound (SMART), providing clear direction and a sense of purpose. Regularly revisiting these goals keeps the team focused and motivated, particularly during the tough phases of the season. Furthermore, cultivating a habit of positive self-talk among your athletes can help them counter negative thoughts and self-doubt, which are often the biggest hurdles in high-stakes competitions.

CREATE A RESILIENT TEAM CULTURE

The culture of a team can significantly influence an athlete's mental toughness. As a coach, you have the power to cultivate an environment that values resilience and mental strength. This involves creating a team identity that prides itself on bouncing back stronger from setbacks and viewing challenges as opportunities to learn and grow. Celebrate efforts and small victories as much as you celebrate wins. Such recognition reinforces the value of persistence and effort over mere outcomes.

Fostering an environment where athletes feel safe to express vulnerabilities is also crucial. When athletes are not afraid to show uncertainty or ask for help, it strengthens the team's cohesion and resilience. Organize team-building activities that are not just fun but also require problem-solving and collaboration under stress. These activities can mimic competition pressures and teach athletes how to work together effectively in stressful situations.

USE OF FEEDBACK AND CONSTRUCTIVE CRITICISM

Feedback is a powerful tool in developing an athlete's mental toughness, but only when used correctly. Constructive criticism helps athletes understand their areas of improvement without feeling diminished or discouraged. Frame feedback in a way that focuses on future improvements rather than past mistakes. For instance, instead of saying, "You didn't handle the pressure well," you might say, "Let's explore some strategies to help you manage pressure better next time."

It's also beneficial to encourage peer-to-peer feedback within the team. When athletes learn to give and receive constructive criticism among themselves, it not only improves their interpersonal skills but also enhances team dynamics. They learn to view feedback as a valuable tool for personal and team improvement, which is essential in building a resilient team.

ROLE-PLAYING AND SCENARIO-BASED TRAINING

Preparing athletes for the mental challenges of competition often involves putting them in simulated pressures of game situations. Role-playing and scenario-based training can be incredibly effective in this regard. For example, setting up a practice where the outcome of the game depends on the last play can simulate end-game pressure. You can also create scenarios where athletes must cope with unexpected changes, such as last-minute lineup changes or unusual referee calls.

These exercises teach athletes to stay mentally engaged and responsive, regardless of the situation, training them to handle real competition stresses more effectively. Moreover, debriefing after these sessions provides valuable insights into how athletes manage stress and pressure, allowing you to tailor your coaching strategies to meet their individual needs more effectively.

By integrating these techniques into your coaching, you help cultivate athletes who are not only strong in body but also in mind, equipped to face the challenges of their sports with resilience and confidence. This holistic approach to coaching not only enhances individual performance but also strengthens the team, making it more competitive and cohesive. As you implement these strategies, observe the transformation in your athletes as they develop into better players and stronger individuals, ready to tackle any challenge on and off the field.

COMMUNICATING EFFECTIVELY WITH YOUNG ATHLETES ABOUT MENTAL HEALTH

In the realm of competitive sports, the dialogue surrounding mental health can often seem like a challenging course to navigate. For coaches, parents, and mentors involved in the development of young athletes, fostering open, honest, and non-judgmental communication is more than just a supportive gesture—it's a fundamental element of nurturing healthy, resilient individuals. Recognizing the importance of mental health and its impact on performance, it's critical to establish and maintain open lines of communication. This ensures that young athletes feel safe and supported in expressing any mental health concerns without fear of stigma or retribution.

In your role as a coach or a parent, think of yourself as a confidant or a trusted advisor, someone who athletes can turn to when the pressures of training, competition, or even personal life seem overwhelming. Regular check-ins can be instrumental. These shouldn't always be formal meetings but can occur during drives home from practice, over a meal, or when setting up for the next game. The key is consistency and the genuine presence you offer during these interactions. Ask open-ended questions that encourage athletes to talk about their feelings and experiences. Phrases like "How did you feel about today's game?" or "What's been on your mind lately with practice?" can open doors to deeper conversations about mental health.

In addition, organizing educational workshops and seminars can play a pivotal role in normalizing conversations about mental health.

These sessions should not only be informative but also engaging and interactive, providing both theoretical and practical knowledge. Bringing in experts such as sports psychologists who can speak on topics ranging from stress management to dealing with performance anxiety adds immense value. These workshops provide a shared learning environment where athletes, along with their coaches and parents, can gain insights into the common mental health challenges athletes face and the best practices to address them. It's also beneficial to include activities that break the ice around mental health discussions, such as role-playing scenarios or group discussions that encourage participants to think and speak openly about these issues.

Choosing appropriate language when discussing mental health is crucial in ensuring that these conversations are productive and supportive. The language used should always be respectful, sensitive, and devoid of any terms that could carry stigma or judgment. For instance, instead of saying someone 'suffers from' a condition, it could be more empowering to say they 'live with' a condition. This subtle shift in language can make a significant difference in how athletes perceive mental health challenges—not as defining traits but as one of the many challenges they might face and manage. It's also important to be specific in your language; vague terms can often be misinterpreted or may not adequately express the gravity or the nature of what the athlete is experiencing.

Encouraging self-expression is another significant aspect of effective communication about mental health. Athletes should be encouraged to express not just their triumphs but also their fears, anxieties, and other feelings they experience in their sporting journey and personal lives. This can be facilitated through various means such as journaling, art, or even music, which provide alternative avenues for expression, especially for those who might find it difficult to articulate their feelings directly. Coaches and parents should be attentive to what is said through these mediums, offering support and guidance when necessary.

By implementing these strategies, you help cultivate an environment where mental health is openly discussed, understood, and prioritized, just like physical health and safety. This approach not only aids in the immediate well-being of young athletes but also equips them with the tools and understanding they need to manage their mental health throughout their lives, both in and out of sports.

THE ROLE OF PARENTS IN DEVELOPING AN ATHLETE'S MENTAL GAME

Creating a supportive home environment is crucial in nurturing a skilled athlete and a well-rounded individual. This support is multifaceted, involving emotional backing, understanding the physical demands, and respecting the psychological pressures of competitive sports. Parents play a pivotal role in shaping this environment, where the mental well-being and confidence of young athletes can flourish. Think of a home where achievements are celebrated; setbacks are seen as learning opportunities and open conversations about challenges are the norm. This kind of environment encourages athletes to remain mentally engaged and resilient in their pursuits. It's about more than just attending games and cheering from the sidelines; it's about providing a consistent foundation that reinforces the mental skills athletes learn in training. This includes recognizing the signs of stress or burnout and having strategies in place to help manage them, ensuring that the home becomes a sanctuary of positivity and encouragement.

Balancing support with avoiding undue pressure is a delicate act but essential for the athlete's development. It's important for parents to encourage their children without pushing them beyond their emotional or physical limits. This balance can be achieved by actively listening to the athlete's needs and responding to them. Encourage open discussions about their goals, the pressures they feel, and how they are managing both successes and failures. This kind of supportive dialogue helps young athletes develop autonomy and make informed decisions about their training, competitions, and overall life balance. It also underscores the importance of recognizing the athlete's individual desires and personal boundaries, which is crucial in fostering a sense of ownership and responsibility over their sports career and personal growth.

Parents can also be involved in their children's training in a way that is constructive and respectful of the coach's role. This involvement should enhance the athlete's experience rather than add pressure or conflict. Attending games and practice sessions is important, but understanding when to step back and allow the coaching staff to guide their performance is equally vital. Constructive involvement also means providing logistical support, such as ensuring they have the necessary equipment and nutrition and helping manage their schedules to avoid overtraining. Parents can also extend their support by learning about the sport's demands and mental challenges, which can foster better communication with both the athlete and the coaching staff. This informed involvement ensures that the support provided at home aligns with the training and goals set in the sporting arena.

Modeling healthy behaviors is perhaps one of the most direct ways parents can influence their athlete's mental game. Children often emulate the behaviors they observe in their parents. Therefore, demonstrating effective stress management, setting realistic goals, and showing resilience in the face of personal challenges serve as live lessons for young athletes. For instance, parents who handle stress through healthy outlets like exercise, reading, or engaging in hobbies show their children practical ways to manage their own stress. Similarly, by setting and pursuing personal goals, parents can exemplify the process of goal-setting, including the planning, effort, setbacks, and adjustments that are part of achieving these goals. When observed and adopted by young athletes, these behaviors can significantly enhance their mental toughness and ability to handle the pressures of competitive sports.

Parents can profoundly impact their child's athletic and personal development through these strategies. By creating a supportive environment, balancing encouragement with pressure, being constructively involved in training, and modeling healthy behaviors, parents lay down a strong psychological foundation. This foundation not only supports the athlete's current sporting endeavors but also instills lifelong skills that enhance their ability to navigate life's challenges with resilience and confidence.

SETTING EXPECTATIONS: THE BALANCE BETWEEN CHALLENGE AND SUPPORT

Setting expectations in sports and athletics is a delicate balance that, when managed correctly, can significantly enhance an athlete's growth and performance. Coaches and parents play a crucial role in helping young athletes set realistic and achievable goals. The importance of this guidance can't be overstated—it fosters motivation and can dramatically influence an athlete's mental approach to training and competition. When setting goals, it's essential to tailor them to the athlete's current abilities while ensuring they are challenging enough to push their limits without causing undue stress or discouragement. For instance, instead of setting a lofty goal of winning a championship early on, it might be more practical to focus on improving specific skills or achieving personal bests. These goals should be clear and measurable, providing a straightforward path for athletes to follow and gauge their progress.

Adapting expectations to fit each athlete's unique needs, abilities, and psychological makeup is another critical aspect of nurturing young sports talents. Every athlete responds differently to training and pressure, influenced by factors like their background, personality, and previous experiences. Some may thrive under high pressure, while others might perform better in a more relaxed environment. Recognizing these differences and adjusting your approach accordingly can make a significant difference in how athletes perceive their abilities and their overall performance. This personalized approach not only helps in setting appropriate challenges but also in crafting a supportive environment that respects each athlete's individual journey.

Effective feedback mechanisms are vital in helping athletes understand where they stand in relation to their goals and what steps they need to take to improve. This feedback should be ongoing and include both formal and informal check-ins. It should be constructive, focusing on specific areas for improvement rather than vague criticisms. For example, if an athlete needs to improve their running technique, specific feedback might involve pointing out the need to maintain a steadier pacing or to adjust their posture. Additionally, involving athletes in the feedback process can be incredibly beneficial. Encouraging them to self-reflect and provide their own insights into their performance fosters a deeper understanding of their skills and a greater sense of responsibility for their development.

Encouraging autonomy in young athletes is perhaps one of the most empowering strategies a coach or parent can employ. When athletes take ownership of their training and development, it boosts their confidence and motivation. This means allowing them the space to make some of their own decisions, whether it's choosing which skills they want to focus on improving or setting their own performance goals. Of course, this autonomy should be guided and supported by coaches and parents to ensure that the choices made are beneficial and aligned with the athletes' overall development plans. Encouraging young athletes to engage actively in their training schedules, goal setting, and even in the strategies for competition days can instill a sense of independence that translates into more confident and self-reliant individuals, both on and off the field.

By focusing on these aspects—setting realistic goals, adapting to individual needs, providing constructive feedback, and fostering autonomy—coaches and parents can effectively support young athletes in their pursuit of excellence. This approach not only helps in building skilled and resilient sports persons but also contributes to their overall growth as confident and self-driven individuals, ready to tackle the challenges of competitive sports with determination and a strong mental foundation.

RECOGNIZING SIGNS OF MENTAL FATIGUE IN ATHLETES

In the competitive world of sports, mental fatigue is an often overlooked condition that can significantly impair a young athlete's performance and overall well-being. Mental fatigue manifests in various symptoms that can subtly creep into an athlete's routine, potentially derailing their training and competitive outcomes.

Common indicators include:

- A noticeable decline in performance.
- A lack of motivation or enthusiasm for the sport.
- Increased irritability with coaches or teammates.
- A marked difficulty in maintaining concentration during practices or events.

These symptoms might be misinterpreted as simple off days or lack of effort, but they are often signs of deeper mental exhaustion.

For coaches and parents, the responsibility of monitoring the well-being of young athletes is paramount. This involves more than just observing their physical performance; it requires attentiveness to changes in their behavior, mood, and overall disposition. Regular check-ins are essential, providing a space for athletes to express how they are feeling about their training, competitions, and any pressures they are experiencing. These conversations should be approached with sensitivity and without judgment, emphasizing the athletes' mental health as a priority. Observational skills are also crucial. Changes such as withdrawal from team interactions, expressions of frustration over minor issues, or decreased enthusiasm during practice sessions can all be indicators of mental fatigue.

When symptoms of mental fatigue are identified, it's crucial to implement interventions that can help athletes recover and regain their mental energy. A key part of these strategies is ensuring adequate rest. Rest should not only be physical but also mental. Encouraging athletes to take complete breaks from sports, where they disconnect entirely from training and competition, can be highly beneficial. During these breaks, engaging in activities unrelated to their sport can help rejuvenate their mind and spirit. This might include hobbies, spending time with friends and family, or simply relaxing. Furthermore, mental breaks such as mindfulness sessions, meditation, or even engaging in light, enjoyable forms of exercise can help clear the mind and reduce stress levels.

Preventative strategies are equally important to help avert the onset of mental fatigue. Proper scheduling of training and competitions is crucial; overtraining is a common cause of mental fatigue, and a well-planned schedule should include adequate periods for rest and recovery. Ensuring that athletes receive enough sleep is also vital, as sleep is essential for cognitive function and emotional health. Nutrition plays a role as well; a diet rich in nutrients supports brain health and overall energy levels. Lastly, maintaining a balanced lifestyle that includes time for social activities, personal interests, and relaxation techniques can help manage stress and prevent mental overload.

By recognizing the signs of mental fatigue early and implementing thoughtful strategies to manage and prevent it, coaches and parents can significantly enhance an athlete's ability to perform at their best both mentally and physically. This proactive approach not only helps in cultivating a healthier, more sustainable athletic career but also instills lifelong habits that support overall well-being.

This chapter has delved into the essential strategies that coaches and parents can employ to foster mental toughness and resilience in young athletes. From effective communication about mental health to recognizing the signs of mental fatigue and intervening appropriately, the approaches outlined here are designed to support the holistic development of athletes. As we move forward, these foundational concepts will serve as pillars for building robust mental toughness strategies that empower athletes to navigate the challenges of their sporting careers with confidence and resilience. Next, we will continue to explore practical techniques and insights that enhance mental toughness, ensuring athletes are equipped to thrive in their pursuits and beyond.

CHAPTER 10
PUTTING IT ALL TOGETHER: STRATEGIES FOR CONTINUOUS IMPROVEMENT

"There may be people that have more talent than you, but there's no excuse for anyone to work harder than you do."
– Derek Jeter

IMAGINE you're preparing for a crucial game. The stakes are high, the crowd is waiting, and you feel the weight of expectation. Now, think about what's going through your mind. Are you worried? Excited? Maybe a bit of both? This is where your mental toughness routine becomes your secret weapon. It's not just about how well you play on the game day but how consistently you prepare your mind and body in the days, weeks, and months leading up to it. In this chapter, we will explore how to develop a personalized mental toughness routine that fits your individual needs and evolves with you, ensuring you stay at the top of your game, no matter what challenges come your way.

DEVELOPING A PERSONALIZED MENTAL TOUGHNESS ROUTINE

Tailor Techniques to Individual Needs

Every athlete is unique—with their own strengths, weaknesses, and personal battles. Therefore, a one-size-fits-all approach to mental training just doesn't cut it. The first step in creating an effective mental toughness routine is to understand and accept your personal athletic profile and psychological makeup. For instance, a sprinter might need to focus intensely for a short period, requiring burst-like mental energy. In contrast, a marathon runner must maintain a steady mental state for hours. Similarly, an introverted athlete might prefer solitary mental exercises, while an extroverted one might thrive on team-based mental toughness activities.

Start by identifying the specific mental challenges you face in your sport. Are you easily distracted? Do nerves get the better of you before a competition? Once you pinpoint these challenges, you can select mental toughness techniques that specifically address them. Techniques can range from visualization, where you mentally rehearse your performance, to cognitive-behavioral strategies that help reframe negative thoughts. Working with a mental coach or a sports psychologist can provide personalized guidance and help you integrate these techniques into a cohesive routine that addresses your specific needs.

CREATING A DAILY MENTAL TOUGHNESS SCHEDULE

Consistency is the backbone of any successful training regimen, and mental training is no exception. Integrating mental toughness exercises into your daily routine ensures they become second nature, empowering you to handle high-pressure situations easily. Schedule short, focused mental training sessions each day. These could be as brief as five minutes of mindfulness meditation in the morning to set a calm, focused tone for the day or ten minutes of journaling in the evening to reflect on your training and mental state.

To effectively incorporate these practices, align them with your existing training schedule. For example, practice breathing exercises during your warm-up to enhance focus, or engage in positive self-talk during cool-downs to reinforce self-belief after a tough training session. The key is to make mental training a regular part of your athletic routine, not something separate or extra. This integration not only improves mental toughness but also enhances overall performance by ensuring mental and physical training complement each other.

INCORPORATING FLEXIBILITY AND ADAPTABILITY

While consistency is crucial, flexibility is equally important. The world of competitive sports is unpredictable—competitions might get rescheduled, unexpected injuries can occur, and personal life events can interfere with training. Your mental toughness routine should be adaptable enough to accommodate these changes without throwing you off your game.

Develop a "mental agility" plan that allows you to modify your mental training according to different scenarios. This might mean having a condensed version of your routine that you can use when time is limited or adjusting the intensity of mental exercises based on your physical training load and competition schedule. Being mentally flexible helps you maintain a high level of preparedness and ensures that your mental toughness does not falter when unexpected changes occur.

UTILIZATION OF TECHNOLOGY AND TOOLS

In today's digital age, numerous apps and tools can help you track and maintain your mental toughness routine. Apps like Headspace provide guided meditation sessions that can be tailored to your schedule and needs, while tools like the Mood Meter help monitor your emotional state, providing insights that can guide your mental training. Additionally, wearable technology can track physiological responses during mental training, giving you concrete data on your progress.

Leveraging these technologies can provide structure and accountability to your mental toughness training, making it easier to track improvements and identify areas needing attention. They also offer the convenience of having your mental training resources readily available, whether you're at home, traveling to a competition, or in a training camp, ensuring that your mental preparation is as mobile and adaptable as your athletic career demands.

Learn how to develop a personalized mental toughness routine that not only addresses your unique needs as an athlete but also seamlessly integrates into your daily life and training. By tailoring techniques to your specific challenges, creating a consistent schedule, maintaining flexibility, and utilizing modern technology, you can ensure that your mental game is as strong and dynamic as your physical performance. Now, let's move forward, ready to tackle the challenges ahead with a mind as well-prepared as your body.

REGULAR SELF-EVALUATION AND ADJUSTMENT OF MENTAL STRATEGIES

Self-evaluation is a pivotal practice in the relentless pursuit of excellence. As an athlete, the ability to introspectively review your mental strategies and their outcomes forms a cornerstone of continuous improvement. Think of it as a regular 'system update' that enhances your mental software, ensuring it runs optimally in every competitive scenario you face. Establishing routine check-ins, whether weekly or monthly, acts as a structured method to assess how effectively your mental strategies are supporting your athletic performance and overall well-being.

During these check-ins, you should focus on several key areas. Performance metrics are crucial; they provide tangible data on how well you are achieving your sports-related goals. However, equally important is the evaluation of your emotional well-being. How are you feeling mentally? Are stress and anxiety levels manageable, or are they hindering your ability to perform? Resilience is another critical area—assess how well you are bouncing back from setbacks and challenges. Are you learning from them, or are they diminishing your confidence and motivation? By addressing these areas, you gain a comprehensive view of what you are achieving and how you are achieving it, which is essential for holistic development.

Adjusting your mental toughness strategies based on the outcomes of these evaluations is where the real growth happens. For example, if you find that pre-competition anxiety is consistently impacting your performance, it might be time to enhance your stress-management techniques, possibly incorporating more advanced methods such as biofeedback or cognitive-behavioral strategies. Feedback from coaches and peers is invaluable during this phase. They can provide an external perspective on your mental toughness, offering insights that you might have overlooked. Maybe your coach notices that your performance dips during high-pressure scenarios, suggesting the need for more targeted pressure simulation training in your routine.

Cultivating a mindset geared towards continuous learning and improvement is crucial. Viewing each evaluation not as a critique but as an opportunity to grow can transform how you approach your mental training. This mindset encourages you to adjust to short-term outcomes and refine and evolve your strategies as you develop as an athlete. It keeps the process dynamic and responsive to your changing needs, ensuring that your mental training remains as rigorous and effective as your physical training.

Remember, the goal of regular self-evaluation is not to critique but to enlighten and guide your path to becoming a mentally tougher, more resilient athlete. By embracing these practices, you ensure that your mental toughness strategies are not static but evolve with you, keeping you prepared and proactive no matter what challenges lie ahead. As you continue to refine your approach, remember that each step, each review, and each adjustment is a stepping stone to greater mental fortitude and, ultimately, superior athletic performance.

STAYING MOTIVATED: RENEWING COMMITMENT TO MENTAL TOUGHNESS GOALS

Motivation is the fuel that drives your journey to maintain and enhance mental toughness. It's what gets you up in the morning for training and pushes you through the last grueling minutes of a workout. But maintaining that drive isn't always easy, especially when faced with the long road of an athletic season or the hurdles of personal development. To keep your mental toughness goals in sharp focus and continuously propel yourself forward, breaking these long-term aspirations into smaller, manageable milestones is crucial. This method makes the goals seem more attainable and provides frequent opportunities to celebrate success, boosting motivation.

Consider setting monthly or even weekly goals that contribute to your overarching objectives. For example, if your main goal is to improve your mental resilience during competitions, a monthly milestone might be to implement specific breathing techniques during all practices within a month. These smaller victories are essential; they not only measure progress but also keep the spirit of achievement alive, making the journey enjoyable and motivating. Each small success builds your confidence and reaffirms your belief in your ability to reach the final goal.

Moreover, incorporating motivational techniques can significantly enhance your commitment. Visualization is a powerful tool; regularly visualizing yourself achieving your goals can embed these aspirations deeply into your subconscious, making them feel more tangible and attainable. Affirmations also play a crucial role. Positive, self-affirming statements repeated daily can remodel your mindset, turning a can-do attitude into a will-do reality. Surrounding yourself with a positive support network—coaches who believe in your potential, teammates who uplift you, and family who support your ambitions—creates an environment ripe for success. This network not only encourages you but also holds you accountable, providing the external push needed when internal motivation wanes.

However, even with strong goals and support, encountering plateaus and setbacks is inevitable. These periods of stagnation can sometimes be demoralizing, but they are also opportunities for significant growth. When progress stalls, revisiting and revising your training methodologies or strategies may be necessary. Engaging in new types of mental training exercises, adjusting your routine, or even seeking feedback from different sources can provide new insights and reinvigorate your approach. Remember, setbacks are not roadblocks but rather stepping stones to greater skill and resilience. Embrace them as part of the process and use them as learning experiences to further fortify your mental toughness.

Lastly, it is important to regularly renew your mental toughness goals, which must be balanced. As you evolve as an athlete, so too should your goals. Every few months, take time to reflect on your current aspirations, celebrate the progress made, and set new targets that align with your growing skills and shifting priorities. This continuous renewal keeps your training aligned with your ultimate athletic ambitions and ensures that your mental toughness regimen remains challenging and effective.

By setting incremental milestones, utilizing motivational techniques, adeptly handling setbacks, and regularly updating your goals, you maintain a dynamic and practical approach to building mental toughness. This ongoing process prepares you to meet the demands of your sport and equips you with the mental resilience necessary for life's various challenges. As we conclude this chapter, remember that the path to mental toughness is a continuous cycle of setting goals, achieving them, learning from the experiences, and setting new challenges. This cycle is crucial not just for your development as an athlete but for your growth as a person. As we move forward, let these strategies be your guide, not just in sports but in every endeavor you undertake.

KEEPING THE GAME ALIVE

Now you have everything you need to boost focus, resilience, and confidence; it's time to pass on your newfound knowledge and show other readers where they can find the same help.

Simply by leaving your honest opinion of this book on Amazon, you'll show other young athletes where they can find the information they're looking for and pass their passion for mental toughness forward.

Thank you for your help. Mental toughness is kept alive when we pass on our knowledge – and you're helping us to do just that.

Scan QR code now to leave your review!

CONCLUSION

AS WE DRAW close to the end of this journey through the landscape of mental toughness for young athletes, it's important to reflect on the foundational role that mental strength plays not just on the field or court, but in every aspect of life. From the classroom to personal relationships, from your spiritual walk to future career paths, the principles of mental toughness we've explored are pivotal. They are the underpinning forces that can propel you toward success and stability in all your endeavors.

Throughout this book, we've navigated a 5-Step Process designed to fortify your mental game. We started by Developing Focus and Concentration, essential for mastering the art of staying present and effective under pressure. Next, we tackled Managing Stress and Anxiety, equipping you with the tools to stay calm and composed. Our journey continued through Building and Sustaining Confidence, where you learned to trust in your abilities and embrace the power of positive self-talk. In Cultivating Resilience and Grit, you discovered the strength to rebound from setbacks stronger than ever. Finally, Balancing Athletics with Life taught you the critical skill of maintaining equilibrium amidst the rigorous demands of being a student-athlete.

Key strategies such as crafting personalized mental routines, engaging in regular self-evaluation, setting adaptive goals, and maintaining open, supportive communication about mental health have been emphasized. These are not just techniques but life skills that will serve you well beyond the sports arena.

In my experience as a physical therapist and personal trainer, I've always advocated for a holistic approach to training. It is essential to remember that your physical and mental capabilities are deeply intertwined—each influencing the other profoundly. As you continue to train your body, remember to nurture your mind with the same vigor and dedication.

The pathway to mental toughness is not static. It's a dynamic journey that demands continuous learning, flexibility, and adaptation. As you grow and face new challenges, the strategies you've learned here will need to be adapted to fit your evolving circumstances and goals.

Now, I urge you to take that first step. Integrate these strategies into your daily routines, commit to continuously developing your mental toughness, and set a course for excellence in all areas of your life.

Let me share a personal anecdote to illustrate this point. Early in my career, I faced a significant setback when an injury threatened to end my athletic pursuits. It was during this challenging time that I truly understood the power of mental resilience. By applying the very principles we've discussed, I not only recovered but returned stronger, eventually running my first marathon, a feat that once seemed impossible. This experience was transformative, teaching me firsthand the incredible impact of mental toughness.

Thank you for joining me on this insightful journey. Your commitment to developing your mental toughness is commendable, and I am confident that the diligence and perseverance you apply today will lead to success in your future athletic endeavors and beyond. Here's to your continued growth, resilience, and excellence in all that you do. Keep pushing, keep striving, and remember—mental toughness is your secret weapon, one that will guide you to achieve remarkable things.

BIBLIOGRAPHY

- Athlete Plus. (n.d.). Mastering time management for student athletes. Retrieved from https://www.athleteplus.org/mastering-time-management-for-student-athletes
- Brandonguyer.com. (n.d.). The ultimate guide to game day routines for athletes. Retrieved from https://brandonguyer.com/blog/the-ultimate-guide-to-game-day-routines-for-athletes
- CHOC. (n.d.). How to prevent burnout in young athletes. Retrieved from https://health.choc.org/how-to-prevent-burnout-in-young-athletes/
- Coaches Toolbox. (n.d.). Positive self-talk for your athletes. Retrieved from https://www.coachestoolbox.net/mental-toughness/positive-self-talk-for-your-athletes
- Competitive Edge. (n.d.). 3 exercises to develop winning concentration. Retrieved from https://www.competitivedge.com/3-exercises-to-develop-winning-concentration/
- Eat Move Hack. (n.d.). Profound impact of diet on mental health. Retrieved from https://www.eatmovehack.com/impact-of-diet-on-mental-health/
- Eventpipe. (2024). 20 great team-building activities for youth sports. Retrieved from https://eventpipe.com/blog/team-building-activities-youth-sports
- Franciscan Media. (n.d.). Mindful breathing. Retrieved from https://www.franciscanmedia.org/pausepray/mindful-breathing/
- Hampden County Physicians. (n.d.). 14 ways Viasil elevates stamina organically. Retrieved from https://hampdencountyphysicians.com/natural-male-enhancement/14-ways-viasil-elevates-stamina-organically/
- Harvard T.H. Chan School of Public Health. (n.d.). Protein. The Nutrition Source. Retrieved from https://nutritionsource.hsph.harvard.edu/what-should-you-eat/protein/
- Human Kinetics. (n.d.). Good communication skills are key to successful coaching. Retrieved from https://us.humankinetics.com/blogs/excerpt/good-communication-skills-are-key-to-successful-coaching
- HuffPost. (n.d.). 3 reasons why failure is the greatest skill to learn from. Retrieved from https://www.huffpost.com/entry/3-reasons-why-failure-is-the-greatest-skill-to-learn_b_58b8b79de4b02eac8876ccc5
- iResearchNet. (n.d.). Mental rehearsal in sport. Retrieved from https://psychology.iresearchnet.com/sports-psychology/psychological-skills/mental-rehearsal-in-sport/
- ISM Health. (2024). Biofeedback therapy: Maximizing performance. Retrieved from https://ismhealth.org/2024/02/biofeedback-therapy-maximizing-performance-for-athletes/
- Law Today Lah. (n.d.). Teen mental health: The impact of positive role models.

130 BIBLIOGRAPHY

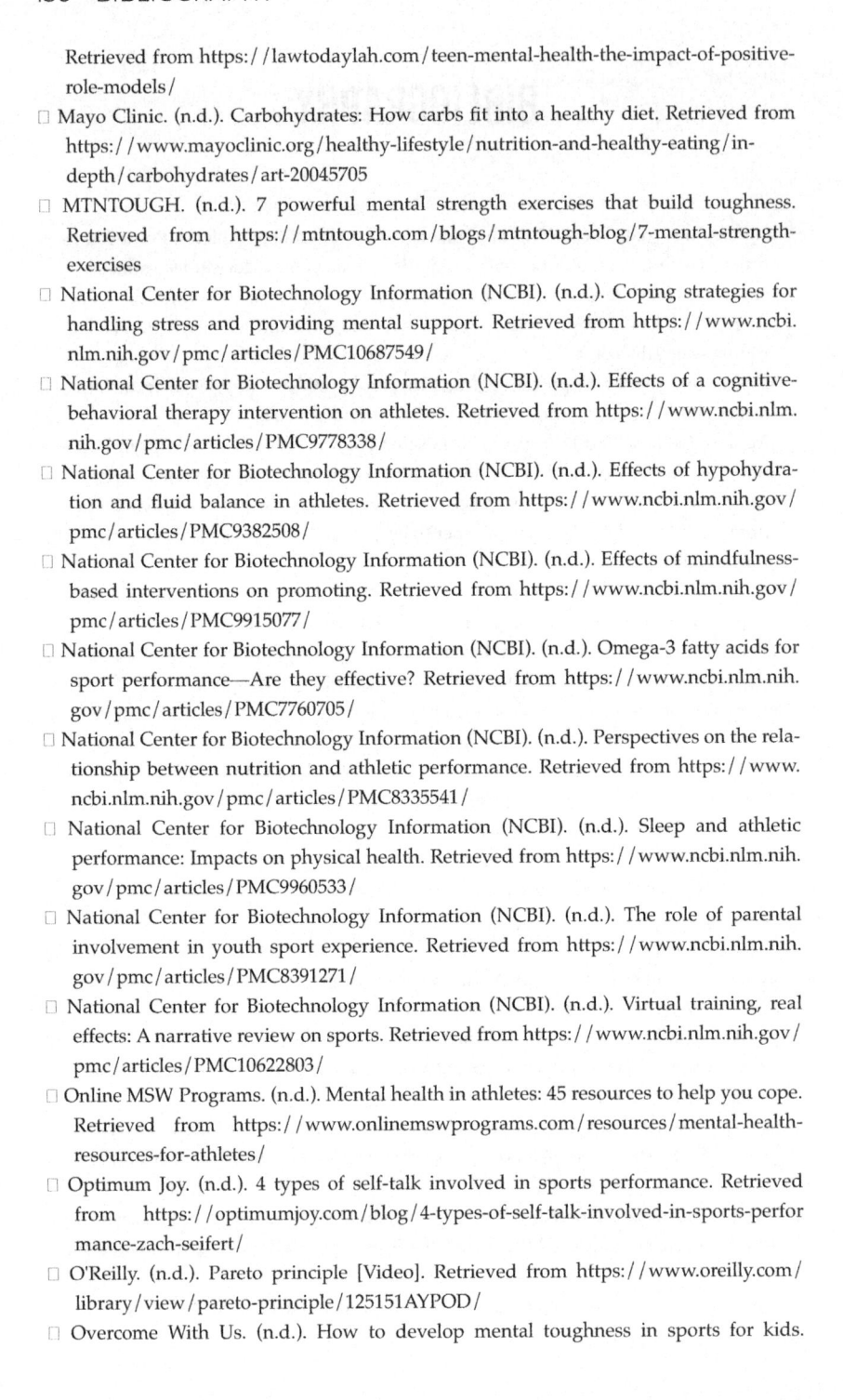

- Retrieved from https://lawtodaylah.com/teen-mental-health-the-impact-of-positive-role-models/
- Mayo Clinic. (n.d.). Carbohydrates: How carbs fit into a healthy diet. Retrieved from https://www.mayoclinic.org/healthy-lifestyle/nutrition-and-healthy-eating/in-depth/carbohydrates/art-20045705
- MTNTOUGH. (n.d.). 7 powerful mental strength exercises that build toughness. Retrieved from https://mtntough.com/blogs/mtntough-blog/7-mental-strength-exercises
- National Center for Biotechnology Information (NCBI). (n.d.). Coping strategies for handling stress and providing mental support. Retrieved from https://www.ncbi.nlm.nih.gov/pmc/articles/PMC10687549/
- National Center for Biotechnology Information (NCBI). (n.d.). Effects of a cognitive-behavioral therapy intervention on athletes. Retrieved from https://www.ncbi.nlm.nih.gov/pmc/articles/PMC9778338/
- National Center for Biotechnology Information (NCBI). (n.d.). Effects of hypohydration and fluid balance in athletes. Retrieved from https://www.ncbi.nlm.nih.gov/pmc/articles/PMC9382508/
- National Center for Biotechnology Information (NCBI). (n.d.). Effects of mindfulness-based interventions on promoting. Retrieved from https://www.ncbi.nlm.nih.gov/pmc/articles/PMC9915077/
- National Center for Biotechnology Information (NCBI). (n.d.). Omega-3 fatty acids for sport performance—Are they effective? Retrieved from https://www.ncbi.nlm.nih.gov/pmc/articles/PMC7760705/
- National Center for Biotechnology Information (NCBI). (n.d.). Perspectives on the relationship between nutrition and athletic performance. Retrieved from https://www.ncbi.nlm.nih.gov/pmc/articles/PMC8335541/
- National Center for Biotechnology Information (NCBI). (n.d.). Sleep and athletic performance: Impacts on physical health. Retrieved from https://www.ncbi.nlm.nih.gov/pmc/articles/PMC9960533/
- National Center for Biotechnology Information (NCBI). (n.d.). The role of parental involvement in youth sport experience. Retrieved from https://www.ncbi.nlm.nih.gov/pmc/articles/PMC8391271/
- National Center for Biotechnology Information (NCBI). (n.d.). Virtual training, real effects: A narrative review on sports. Retrieved from https://www.ncbi.nlm.nih.gov/pmc/articles/PMC10622803/
- Online MSW Programs. (n.d.). Mental health in athletes: 45 resources to help you cope. Retrieved from https://www.onlinemswprograms.com/resources/mental-health-resources-for-athletes/
- Optimum Joy. (n.d.). 4 types of self-talk involved in sports performance. Retrieved from https://optimumjoy.com/blog/4-types-of-self-talk-involved-in-sports-performance-zach-seifert/
- O'Reilly. (n.d.). Pareto principle [Video]. Retrieved from https://www.oreilly.com/library/view/pareto-principle/125151AYPOD/
- Overcome With Us. (n.d.). How to develop mental toughness in sports for kids.

Retrieved from https://overcomewithus.com/parenting/how-to-develop-mental-toughness-in-sports-for-kids
- Performance Psychology Center. (n.d.). Visualization techniques and mental imagery for athletes. Retrieved from https://www.performancepsychologycenter.com/post/visualization-techniques-and-mental-imagery
- Plant Prana Essential Oils. (n.d.). Clinical corner: Sleep. Retrieved from https://www.plantpranaoils.com/clinical-corner-sleep/
- PositivePsychology.com. (n.d.). Boosting mental toughness in young athletes & 20. Retrieved from https://positivepsychology.com/mental-toughness-for-young-athletes/
- Productive Recruit. (n.d.). The ultimate guide to SMART goals for student-athletes. Retrieved from https://productiverecruit.com/blog/smart-goals-for-student-athletes
- Rapids Youth Soccer. (n.d.). The power of role models. Retrieved from https://rapidsyouthsoccer.org/news/front-page-news/the-power-of-role-models/
- Resilience Institute. (n.d.). 10 inspiring examples of highly resilient sportspeople. Retrieved from https://resiliencei.com/blog/10-inspiring-examples-of-highly-resilient-sportspeople
- SIRC. (n.d.). Overcoming setbacks: Developing resilience. Retrieved from https://sirc.ca/blog/overcoming-setbacks-developing-resilience/
- SkillShark. (n.d.). 5 reasons why athlete self-assessments improve performance. Retrieved from https://skillshark.com/athlete-self-assessments-improve-performance/
- Strength Counselling. (2023, July 23). 4 effective ways to change your negative mindset. Retrieved from https://strengthcounselling.ca/2023/07/23/change-your-negative-mindset/
- Success Starts Within. (n.d.). Sports visualization techniques for athletes. Retrieved from https://www.successstartswithin.com/sports-psychology-articles/visualization-for-sports/visualization-techniques-for-athletes/
- Sunday Vision. (n.d.). Discover the 4-7-8 breathing technique that makes you fall asleep in just one minute. Retrieved from https://www.sundayvision.co.ug/discover-the-4-7-8-breathing-technique-that-makes-you-fall-asleep-in-just-one-minute/
- Texas State University News. (2023). For college athletes, success hinges on balancing. Retrieved from https://news.txst.edu/research-and-innovation/2023/collegiate-student-athlete-success-hinges-on-balancing-demands.html
- The Behaviour Institute. (n.d.). Goal-setting secrets in sports psychology. Retrieved from https://thebehaviourinstitute.com/maximizing-performance-uncover-goal-setting-secrets-in-sports-psychology/
- TrainingPeaks. (n.d.). How to cultivate a growth mindset in athletes. Retrieved from https://www.trainingpeaks.com/coach-blog/how-to-cultivate-a-growth-mindset-in-athletes
- TrueSport. (n.d.). 3 reasons why your athlete needs healthy boundaries. Retrieved from https://truesport.org/decision-making/3-reasons-why-your-athlete-needs-

healthy-boundaries/#:~:text=Remember%2C%20the%20first%20step%20to,their%20own%20feelings%20as%20well.
- UCHealth. (n.d.). Why rest and recovery is essential for athletes. Retrieved from https://www.uchealth.org/today/rest-and-recovery-for-athletes-physiological-psychological-well-being/
- Williamsburg Times. (n.d.). The connection between physical and mental well-being. Retrieved from https://wbach.net/the-connection-between-physical-and-mental-well-being-2/
-Youth Sports Psychology. (n.d.). Helping kids build resiliency in sports. Retrieved from https://www.youthsportspsychology.com/youth_sports_psychology_blog/helping-kids-build-resiliency-in-sports/

ABOUT THE AUTHOR

Rush Hemphill is a physical therapist, personal trainer and author, dedicated to promoting physical wellness and health education. As a seasoned professional in the fitness industry, Rush has cultivated a deep understanding of the vital role physical activity plays in maintaining overall health.

With experience in both personal training and physical therapy, he advocates for a holistic approach to fitness, emphasizing the importance of both physical and mental well-being. Rush's approach to fitness is not just about achieving short-term goals but fostering a sustainable and balanced lifestyle.

His passion for fitness and health education has led him to author several influential books on these subjects. These books offer practical advice, innovative training and workout routines, mindset, and insights into injury prevention and rehabilitation. Rush's writing is known for its clarity, making complex fitness concepts accessible to a wide audience.

Rush's mission is to inspire people of all ages and fitness levels to embrace a more active lifestyle. He believes that physical activity should be a joyful and integral part of daily life, not a chore. Through his books and coaching, he aims to empower individuals to take charge of their physical health, enhance their quality of life, and find joy in movement.

ALSO BY RUSH HEMPHILL

Train like a Hybrid Athlete: Optimize your health, fitness and performing with running and strength training. 4-week training

The Essentials of Strength Training for Seniors: A Simple Guide to Increase Strength, Balance, and Mobility to Promote Longevity and Improve Independence

Made in the USA
Las Vegas, NV
14 October 2024